The Dangerous Kind

Graeme Sellers

For my father, the most dangerous man I ever knew.

"He's stirring up unrest among the people with his teaching, disturbing the peace everywhere, starting in Galilee and now all through Judea.

He's a dangerous man, endangering the peace."

—LUKE 23:5

Contents

Living Dangerously in a Perilous Time   1

The Naturally Supernatural Life   17

A Dangerous Kindness   29

The Spirit and the Mind   47

Under the Word   59

Hiddenness   77

Love: God's Gold Standard   93

Repent—Kingdom Life Starts Here   109

Reckless   123

This is the Key to Your Life   147

Living Dangerously in A Perilous Time

Too long have followers of Jesus settled for religious compliance and inoffensive comportment. Too long have rank and file Christians delegated the dangerous life of following Jesus to the professionals, believing them best suited for the radical engagement with the world that Jesus models. Too long have we believed that the highest goal of Christianity is conforming people to good behavior, getting folks to follow the rules, making people nice.

Now is the time to raise our danger quotient.

Now is the time for us to move from bland church drones into followers of the living Christ who are potent for the purposes of God and a mortal threat to the enemy of our souls.

Many of us have lived with far lower expectations of our place in the scheme of things. We do not think of ourselves as a threat to Satan or as possessors of spiritual potency bringing hope, freedom, and life to those living in darkness. We see our constant and frequently unsuccessful struggle with our baser nature and cannot imagine winning a wrestling match with dark angels. We acknowledge our faltering faith and cannot envision walking in the kind of power of God that moves mountains. We're ordinary, seemingly inconsequential people doing our best to get by. The idea that we are made to be dangerous, as alluring as it is, sounds absurd to our ears.

But the reality of our calling and identity—as God defines and declares it—is vastly different than the smallness of our vision for our own lives. The truth is, all who call on the name of Jesus are thrust into the heart of a cosmic conflict in which the stakes are ultimate: life and death. We do not follow Jesus for our own amusement, nor merely to secure our own salvation. We follow him because he is altogether lovely and in him is eternal and abundant life, and he has commissioned us to be about the work he gave his life to.

Before returning to the Father, Jesus gave this charge to his disciples: "God authorized and commanded me to commission you: Go out and train everyone you meet, far and near, in this way of life, marking them by baptism in the threefold name: Father, Son, and Holy Spirit. Then instruct them in the practice of all I have commanded you" (Matthew 28:18b-20a MSG).

The implication is unmistakable. We have no other mission than the ministry of Jesus. A lesser job description will not do. In fact, a lesser job description is unbiblical. His work is to be ours, and it is singularly summarized by John this way: "Now the Son of God came to earth with the express purpose of liquidating the devil's activities" (1 John 3:8b PHILLIPS). Destroying the work of the devil is the heart of kingdom ministry, and to this our lives are to be given.

Two questions arise. First: if Jesus defeated Satan utterly on the cross and through his resurrection,[1] haven't the devil's works already been destroyed? If so, is there anything left for us to do? This is a vexing query, because while the Bible clearly states that Jesus

---

[1] Numerous scriptures describe Satan's defeat by Jesus; among them are Colossians 2:15 AMP: "[God] disarmed the principalities and powers that were ranged against us and made a bold display and public example of them, in triumphing over them in Him and in it [the cross]"; Hebrews 2:14b NLT: "only by dying could he break the power of the Devil, who had the power of death"; 1 Peter 3:22 NLT: "Now Christ has gone to heaven. He is seated in the place of honor next to God, and all the angels and authorities and powers are bowing before him."

defeated Satan, we can see for ourselves that much evil yet abounds in this world. What are we to make of this?

Swiss theologian Oscar Cullman offers the analogy of D-Day to explain the tension of Satan's defeat and the ongoing activity of the evil one. On D-Day during World War Two, Europe was invaded and the battle shifted inalterably in the Allies' favor. In a sense, the war was won on June 6, 1944, even though there were long months of warfare and bloodshed to come. Christ's incarnation and death at Calvary represent D-Day, but we await the final consummation of the war against evil when Jesus comes again. Until then we live "between the times," in an age in which Christ's victory and Satan's dying endeavors overlap.[2]

In other words, there is still formidable warfare to be fought by the followers of Jesus, an ongoing battle against the powers of hell. The dangerous kind are a threat to the enemy precisely because they recognize that the battle is real and must be waged in the power of the Holy Spirit.

The second question, then: given the reality of evil in our world, and given that we have no other ministry than the ministry of Jesus, what is our present role in destroying the works of the devil? What does it look like? What exactly are we to be doing?

First we must understand what the works of the devil are. A contemporary theologian proposes six categories of Satan's activity on earth:[3]

- *Morally*, Satan entices to sin.
- *Physically*, he inflicts disease and death.
- *Intellectually*, he seduces into error.
- *Socially*, he provokes hatred and chaos.
- *Politically and Economically*, he produces injustice and oppression.

---

[2] O. Cullman, *Christ and Time: The Primitive Christian Conception of Time and History*, F. V. Filson, trans. (London: SCM Press, Ltd., 1951), 84.

[3] Sam Storm, "Defeat of Devil-Demons," Enjoying God Ministries, November 8, 2006, http://enjoy. monkcms.net (accessed March 2, 2009).

- *Spiritually*, he blinds the minds of unbelievers to the truth of the gospel.

Jesus describes the goal of his earthly ministry as seeking and saving what was lost.[4] Jesus' ministry is fundamentally one of reversing Satan's inroads. We follow in Jesus' footsteps—we do his ministry—when we oppose every scheme of the adversary and invite kingdom breakthrough wherever darkness holds sway. So, our kingdom work meets the enemy's head-on in each category:

- *Morally*, we encourage people into the true freedom and joy of living within the protective boundaries of God's standards. Of their sin, we say with the Father's compassion, "That doesn't look good on you," and we commend to them the beauty of Christ's righteousness.
- *Physically*, we pray boldly and obediently for physical healing, release from demonic strongholds, and the raising of the dead.
- *Intellectually*, we graciously speak and present the truth that sets men and women free.
- *Socially*, we contend for vibrant, healthy relationships and an unconditional love for all people.
- *Politically and Economically*, we defend the poor, the widows, and the marginalized, administrating heaven's justice as God's ambassadors on earth.
- *Spiritually*, we bring light into the darkness, inviting and welcoming people into a saving relationship with Jesus Christ.

Clearly this is a departure from an understanding of Christianity that spends itself on keeping the local church going. In fact, the kingdom ministry of destroying Satan's works may have very little to do with the typical activities of the traditional church.

---

[4] Luke 19:10. See also the variant reading of Luke 9:56 NKJV, "For the Son of Man did not come to destroy men's lives but to save them."

4

For years most of our Christian activity has been church-centered, and our service to God was weighed by how much we did on behalf of our local fellowship. We've contented ourselves with being somewhat moral, going to church, and helping our church become more successful. This is a far cry from being dangerous. Our understanding of God's activity and call must expand beyond the walls of the local church. Becoming dangerous entails moving from church to kingdom in our thinking and acting.

Kingdom ministry focused on loosening the devil's hold depends in no small measure on understanding the times. Destroying the devil's works follows a conviction that not only are we to be about the ministry of Jesus, but also that the dark days we live in demand our uncompromising willingness to wage the good warfare.

Do we understand, soberly and personally, the time we are in? Jesus adjures us to recognize the signs of the times and to align our lives accordingly. "When evening comes, you say, 'It will be fair weather, for the sky is red,' and in the morning, 'Today it will be stormy, for the sky is red and overcast.' You know how to interpret the appearance of the sky, but you cannot interpret the signs of the times" (Matthew 16:3 NIV).

In these days having excellent ministry skills is not enough. Attending conferences, reading books, and holding 24-hour prayer meetings are insufficient. All of these can be helpful, but none are adequate for the task at hand. The task is dangerous living, existing from the radical missionary call of Christ, risking everything for the sake of the King who called us out of the darkness into his marvelous light. It is a hazardous enterprise because we do not go forward unopposed.

As the time of Christ's return draws nearer, the efforts of our adversary are redoubled. And yet, so many behave as if it's business as usual, as if strengthening the institutional church by increasing the ABCs—attendance, buildings, cash—is the highest thing we can give ourselves to. Though the times are perilous, we conduct ourselves as though we live in a time of peace and consider Satan, if he exists at all, a toothless gremlin not meriting serious response. We would do well to heed C. S. Lewis, who noted, "There are two equal and opposite errors into which our race can fall about the devils. One is to disbelieve in their existence. The other is to believe, and to feel an excessive and unhealthy interest in them. They themselves are equally pleased by both errors."[5]

Our interest is not in the enemy and his ilk, but in the surpassing greatness of knowing Christ. He alone commands our fascination. Knowing Christ requires us both to embrace his mission as our own and to understand our identity as warriors in a dark time who have been called to noble and high purposes.

It is written into the hearts of men and women to give themselves to greatness, to live lives of authentic and enduring significance. When we are denied this our courage atrophies and our hearts despair. In the midst of the pedestrian activities of everyday life, our spirit urges us, "Surely we're made for something more." Abraham Lincoln, one of the greatest American presidents, endured a suicidal depression twenty years before taking office, and would have gladly died except that "he had done nothing to make any human being remember that he had lived." Lincoln's biographer relates, "As a young man, Abraham Lincoln worried that the 'field of glory' had been harvested by the founding fathers, that nothing had been left for his generation but modest ambitions."[6]

We no less than Lincoln wonder the same. Is there greatness left to attempt for our King? Are there noble kingdom deeds to give ourselves to? Emerging as we are from a century of unrivaled church growth,[7] we may well ask whether the great advances of

---

[5] C. S. Lewis, *The Screwtape Letters* (New York: Macmillan, 1962), 3.

[6] Doris Kearns Goodwin, *Team of Rivals: The Political Genius of Abraham Lincoln* (New York: Simon & Schuster, 2005), 501; xix. Only upon issuing the Emancipation Proclamation could Lincoln confidently say that he had left a mark of lasting significance.

[7] According to David B. Barrett and Todd M. Johnson (*World Christian Trends AD 30-AD 2000: Interpreting the Annual Christian Megacensus* [Pasadena, CA.: William Carey Library, 2001], 19 and 551), the church grew more in the twentieth century than in all the previous nineteen centuries since the time of Christ combined, with almost two billion adherents worldwide.

God's kingdom have already been made. So we wonder: is there anything left to our generation but modest ambitions?

The answer, Paul explains to Timothy, is a resounding *"Yes!"* We have been called to the great warfare of our time.

> This charge I commit to you, son Timothy, according to the prophecies previously made concerning you, that by them you may wage the good warfare, holding fast to faith (that leaning of the entire human personality on God in absolute trust and confidence) and having a good (clear) conscience (1 Timothy 1:18-19a NKJV, AMP).

Summoned to War

The days are dark and dangerous, and so with Timothy we have been summoned to war by the One who commands the angel armies of heaven. This is not mere metaphor, nor the romantic language of the heroic quest, and those who assume so do so at their peril. Jesus makes this clear. Satan, the father of lies, comes *only* to steal and kill and destroy (John 8:44, 10:10). Peter reinforces this in his letter to persecuted Christians in Rome and Asia. "Be careful!" he tells them. "Watch out for attacks from the Devil, your great enemy. He prowls around like a roaring lion, looking for some victim to devour" (1 Peter 5:8 NLT).

It's unlikely we truly believe either Peter or Jesus. The familiarity of the words dulls our attentiveness, and we consign the imagery to imaginative vocabulary rather than to the realm of literal reality. This relegation both fits our rationalistic worldview and demands far less of us personally. John Calvin, a French theologian during the Protestant Reformation, commenting on Paul's exhortation to Timothy, writes, "The greater part wish to serve Christ at ease, and as if it were pastime, whereas Christ calls all his servants to warfare."[8]

---

[8] John Calvin, *Commentary on 1 Timothy*, WORDsearch 9 Bible software, build 9.0.2.125.

But allegiance to Jesus Christ is not something we can squeeze in between all the other things we have to do. It's not just a Sunday thing, should we manage to roll out of bed in time to make it to church. According to Paul we are soldiers summoned to war against an adversary whose goal is our total defeat. Sometimes he sneaks up on cat's paws, seducing us into carelessness, self-indulgence, or indifference; sometimes we face an all-out, full-frontal assault. Either way, Scripture unambiguously tells us that the war is real and we have been conscripted to fight the battle.

For too long too many Christians have little resembled well trained warriors in a cosmic conflict and too much resembled the Cambridge ladies of e. e. cummings celebrated sonnet, women who are altogether occupied with trivialities rather than the unbounded possibilities of life.

> the Cambridge ladies who live in furnished souls
> are unbeautiful and have comfortable minds
> (also, with the church's protestant blessings
> daughters, unscented shapeless spirited)
> they believe in Christ and Longfellow, both dead,
> are invariably interested in so many things —
> at the present writing one still finds
> delighted fingers knitting for the is it Poles?
> perhaps. While permanent faces coyly bandy
> scandal of Mrs. N and Professor D
> . . . the Cambridge ladies do not care, above
> Cambridge if sometimes in its box of
> sky lavender and cornerless, the
> moon rattles like a fragment of angry candy[9]

Cummings's complaint is against disinterested people who "do not think for themselves,...who spend their days in pursuits which never fully engage them, who approach real passion only with a snicker, and who are completely unaware of anything larger than

---

[9] e. e. cummings, *Complete Poems 1913-1962* (New York: Harcourt Brace Jovanovich, 1980), 70.

themselves."[10] Jesus voiced a similar complaint about men who strictly followed religious rituals but missed the point of the whole enterprise: a vital friendship with the God of the universe. "You have your heads in your Bibles constantly because you think you'll find eternal life there," Jesus observes (John 5:39-40, 42, 44 MSG), "But you miss the forest for the trees. These Scriptures are all about *me*! And here I am, standing right before you, and you aren't willing to receive from me the life you say you want....I know you and your crowds. I know that love, especially God's love, is not on your working agenda....How do you expect to get anywhere with God when you spend all your time jockeying for position with each other, ranking your rivals and ignoring God?"

His indictment of their lives is ruthless. "Alas for you, you hypocritical scribes and Pharisees! You are like white-washed tombs, which look fine on the outside but inside are full of dead men's bones and all kinds of rottenness. For you appear like good men on the outside—but inside you are a mass of pretence and wickedness" (Matthew 23:27-28 PHILLIPS).

Jesus takes no satisfaction in leveling these charges. In fact, it deeply distresses him that instead of embracing the passionate, dangerous life available to them, they have ended up not knowing God and opposing his purposes. As a result, not only they but all who follow them have been rendered spiritually impotent. "Jerusalem, Jerusalem!" he laments (Matthew 23:37 HCSB), "The city who kills the prophets and stones those who are sent to her. How often I wanted to gather your children together, as a hen gathers her chicks under her wings, yet you were not willing!"

Against this backdrop we understand that we can afford no more half-awake endeavors, no more half-hearted commitment, no more halfway measures. Now is the day we must go all the way through, the time we become dangerous people for the Lord, and answer Paul's exhortation to *"wage the good warfare."*

---

[10] Teresa Gibson, *e.e. cummings' 'Daughters of the Church' as St. Paul's 'tinkling cymbals,'* http://blue.utb. edu (accessed March 15, 2009).

The charge, as Paul issues it, has three components: God's unique call on our lives, the specific command he issues to all of us, and our commitment to see it through to the end.

The Call

Living dangerously begins with God's call on each person's life. That's where Paul begins with Timothy, with what God has spoken over and into Timothy's life. Paul could have started elsewhere. Timothy was his pastoral protégé; Paul might have based his injunction to Timothy on his intimate knowledge of Timothy's skills, his personal assessment of Timothy's character, or his approval of Timothy's advanced spiritual training regimen (which Paul had designed himself). But he does not. Had he so chosen, Paul's instructions to Timothy could have been predicated on their friendship; after all, no one knew better than Paul Timothy's heart, hopes, and aspirations. He could have written, "Based on everything I know about you, Timothy, and all that I have seen in you, this is what I think you should do." But he does not. His injunction to Timothy is established on the basis of what God has spoken concerning the young pastor's life.

God's words, not human words, will commission Timothy into the great warfare of his time. So, too, are we summoned. Not by chance but by design. Not by human hunches but by divine decree. Not by evaluation of our fitness by experts, but by God's understanding of our weaknesses and his decision to use us in the midst of them. Only this way shall we enter into dangerous living: by the word of God and the call of God over our lives. We are, each of us, summoned to war, to live dangerously: *"You are a man who has been chosen and you cannot refuse your task."[11]*

---

[11] William Barclay, the summary of Paul's charge, in *The Daily Study Bible*, WORDsearch 9 Bible software, build 9.0.2.125.

"According to the prophecies previously made concerning you," is how Paul puts it to Timothy. This is the rocket fuel launching Timothy into his destiny: a personal, prophetic declaration from the God who designed Timothy's destiny and who knew him when he was in his mother's womb. Earlier in his ministry Paul had laid hands on Timothy and imparted a spiritual gift; the council of elders had done so too, with the impartation of a gift following (2 Timothy 1:6; 1:14). Were either of these the occasion for the prophecies spoken over Timothy? We can only guess. But what we know with certainty is that the Lord had designated Timothy for assignment with life-specific words of direction and encouragement. Could anything be a more compelling, more persuasive call to dangerous living?

But what if, unlike Timothy, we've never received a personal word, a prophecy concerning our future, a heaven-sent dream? Are we spiritual exceptions, 4-F rejects who cannot be conscripted into the purposes of the Lord in these darkening days? Hardly. Though prophetic words and impartations are wonderful to receive, and though in some circles such experiences are held up as badges of honor, they do not establish our kingdom worth. Nor does the lack of such experiences invalidate our call to dangerous living in kingdom ministry. For all have a call, a call issued by the one enthroned in heaven. "Long ago, even before he made the world, God loved us and chose us in Christ," Paul assures his friends in Ephesus. "For we are God's masterpiece, created in Christ Jesus to do good works, which God prepared in advance for us to do" (Ephesians 1:4, 2:10 NLT, NIV).

This is the basis of our summons and of God's confidence in us: he knew us before the foundations of the earth were laid and appointed a glorious field for us to harvest!

The Command

> This charge I commit to you, son Timothy, according to the prophecies previously made concerning you, that by them you may wage the good warfare, holding fast to faith (that leaning of the entire human personality on God in absolute trust and confidence) and having a good (clear) conscience (1 Timothy 1:19a NKJV, AMP).

Paul's specific command to Timothy, "wage the good warfare," has two essential elements. Notably, Paul exerts no effort attempting to persuade Timothy the war is real, nor that he's been called into it. These are accepted, undisputed realities. Both Timothy and the broader church audience who will read this letter know all too well that in the present cosmic conflict, they will either fight or die. Rather, he specifies how kingdom people are to approach their assignment.

First, we are to hold fast to the faith. This means, simply, that even when things are darkest and hardest, we "lean the entire human personality on God in absolute trust and confidence." We wage warfare not on the basis of our abilities, nor on a sense of our worthiness to be used by God, but from a conviction of God's surpassing greatness and excellence. This is no minor detail, especially for those who tend to disqualify themselves from significant kingdom ministry for shortcomings both real and imagined. The starting point is God, not our competencies and deficiencies, which is why Paul insists that we lean wholly on the father of Jesus, trusting his kindness and power to find expression through us.

Second, we venture into this adventure with a clear conscience. A clear conscience follows from intimate friendship with Jesus, knowing the wonder of his person more clearly and the beauty of his forgiveness more personally, and moved by a desire to enjoy the life he offers. This is the underpinning of a clear conscience.

It comes not from rigorous attempts to conform our own behavior but from glad agreement with his purposes and standards for our lives. Clear conscience is pure gift, a Spirit-breathed marvel of renewal that propels us to order our actions so they line up with God's desires for us. Behavior is part of it, of course, but not the primary part. Intimacy and joy are the main ingredients of a clear conscience because the happy heart that has found friendship with God lives freely and easily in his grace. Here our fascination is continually with our Lord and Friend, not with ourselves and taking our spiritual temperature.

Holding fast to the faith and having a clear conscience are prerequisites for effectiveness on the battlefield. The command itself, "wage the good warfare," leads us into the good, kingdom life. In fact, living the good, kingdom life **is** waging the good, kingdom warfare. And what is the good life in Christ? Nothing less than his mission and ministry made real in our world. It is as simple as an act of compassion prompted by the Spirit. It is as basic as giving a cup of water to the thirsty. It is as uncomplicated as a word of encouragement at just the right moment to the person who needs it. It is as ordinary as praying for someone who's sick. It is as unforced as welcoming a stranger. This is how the kingdom advances, and every time compassion and healing move forth the darkness retreats.

These are laudable things to do, certainly, but are they truly weapons? Paul would contend that they are. "The very weapons we use are not those of human warfare," he acknowledges, "but [are] powerful in God's warfare for the destruction of the enemy's strongholds" (2 Corinthians 10:4 PHILLIPS).

The Commitment

Paul insists we not lose our focus, nor allow ourselves to get distracted. "No one serving in the army gets entangled in everyday affairs," he writes, "The soldier's aim is to please the enlisting officer" (2 Timothy 2:4 NRSV). We cannot afford to become encumbered by nonessential activity; we cannot indulge meaningless endeavors that do not threaten the darkness.

Nor can we risk relaxing, assuming the good warfare has been fought and finished. "Life is one long campaign," William Barclay reminds us, "A service from which there is no release, not a short, sharp struggle after which a man can lay aside his arms and rest in peace....It is there that the danger enters in. It is necessary to be forever on the watch....It is one of the commonest dangers in life to proceed in a series of spasms. We must remember that we are summoned to a campaign which goes on as long as life does."[12]

The Stakes Have Been Raised

This is the clarion call in a dark time: church as usual will not cut it; we must become revolutionaries in a religious age.

An overstatement? Consider that every letter to the seven churches in Revelation has a reference to overcoming and that in the New Testament, "overcome" is a spiritual warfare word. *Nikaó*, "to conquer, overcome," always assumes the conflict between God or Christ and the opposing demonic powers.[13] We may not like that warfare is our lot, but this does not excuse us from the battle that is before us.

In J. R. R. Tolkien's fantasy masterpiece *The Lord of the Rings,* the great battle of the ages has come to Middle Earth. King Theoden is none too eager to engage in it. He says to Aragorn, "I would not risk open war." Aragorn replies plainly, "Open war is upon you, whether you would risk it or not."[14]

---

[12] Barclay, summary.

[13] Walther Günther, *The New International Dictionary of New Testament Theology,* Vol. 1 (Grand Rapids, MI: Zondervan Publishing House, 1975), 650.

[14] *The Lord of the Rings, The Two Towers*, Peter Jackson, director, based on the novel by J. R. R. Tolkein (New Line Cinema, 2002).

Open war is upon the followers of Jesus whether we would risk it or not. As we pursue our dangerous destiny, may this encouragement from C. H. Spurgeon strengthen our resolve: "Beloved, a life of warfare is before us, but the Lord of Hosts is with us."[15]

---

[15] C. H. Spurgeon, *Faith's Checkbook*, Devotional for April 18, http://www.lightsource.com/devotionals/faiths-checkbook-by-ch-spurgeon/faiths-checkbook-april-18-11538361-11538361.html (accessed November 9, 2011).

The Naturally Supernatural Life

Freedom. Danger. Destiny.

We were made for these. Made for life on the wild side with Christ the Conqueror, thrust into an adventure of epic proportions in which we experience the kingdom of God breaking through in our words, dreams, actions. The life we were made for is Christ's own daring mission, the good warfare, which he described this way:

> The Spirit of the Lord [is] upon Me, because He has anointed Me [the Anointed One, the Messiah] to preach the good news (the Gospel) to the poor; He has sent Me to announce release to the captives and recovery of sight to the blind, to send forth as delivered those who are oppressed [who are downtrodden, bruised, crushed, and broken down by calamity], To proclaim the accepted and acceptable year of the Lord [the day when salvation and the free favors of God profusely abound] (Luke 4:18-19 AMP).

We have settled for a narrower, anesthetized life, believing our lot to be a lesser destiny. That Jesus would do the outrageous things he proposed is no surprise; after all, he's God-in-the-flesh visiting a broken planet and he walks in the power of heaven itself. Of course *he* resurrects the dying hopes of the poor with a message of relentless life. Of course *his* touch is electric with healing, shattering the hold of sickness, disease, and the demonic. Of course *he* rends the darkness with unapproachable light and causes "the free favors of God to profusely abound." You can do those sorts of things when you're God.

The rest of us are, well, something other. Exactly what, we're not quite sure, but we know this: there's only one Jesus, and we're not him. His ministry—his life direction, passion, calling, and activity—is exactly that: his. And ours? Who can say for sure? One thing seems clear: our trajectory will be lower and lesser. After all, we are mere mortals.

The psalmist makes a parallel observation. He says we were created a touch lower than the angels, a little less than God (Psalm 8:5). The poet is struck by God's condescension to humankind, God's glad willingness to entrust dominion over the created order to men and women. It is woven into creation's design that we would have a here-and-now, this-world responsibility. We are given charge over the birds of the air, the fish of the sea, the cattle of the field. The natural world is our domain and, as the psalmist notes, this is an incomprehensible innovation. Why would God so regard humanity? Why would God's love so confidently and freely give such jurisdiction to bumblers and amateurs like us? It's a mystery. The psalmist is reduced to wonder and praise. "O Lord, our Lord," he cries (Psalm 8:9 AMP), "How excellent (majestic and glorious) is Your name in all the earth!"

Our part, as we understand the poet, is limited to the natural world. Jesus' life, by contrast, effortlessly traverses the gridlines of the natural realm into the supernatural. This makes perfect sense, given his unique nature as the one who is fully God and fully human. It makes sense too that we would assume only Jesus moves between the two realms. We are caretakers of the natural order; Jesus is a barrier breaker into the supernatural. Consequently, we're inclined to believe the supernatural works of Jesus are off limits to us. At best ours is a shadow ministry of his, a grape juice version of his premium vintage new wine.

This may be our perspective, perhaps even our experience, but it runs counter to Jesus' own expectation of what our lives will look like when we are fully committed to following him. The Son of Man recognizes no restriction of our influence and activity to the natural world. He will not endorse the limitations of our lives that we've resigned ourselves to. His dreams for us are off the map, and that's where he instructs us to go.

"Very truly, I tell you," Jesus informs his friends, "the one who believes in me will also do the works that I do and, in fact, will do greater works than these, because I am going to the Father" (John 14:12 NRSV).

His statement runs counter to our outlook. And for most of us it does not line up with the reality of our Christian lives. Greater works than Jesus? It confounds the mind and the heart. Jesus did all the heavy lifting—living a sinless life, suffering the cruelest capital punishment on our behalf, standing death on its head. Reason suggests all that's left is some mopping up, spiritual scut work requiring little expertise or heavenly intervention. Lesser works than Jesus, that's what we'd expect him to commission.

But he doesn't.

The question is, why not? Given our inherent weakness, brokenness, and sinfulness, why would Jesus cast a vision for us as barrier breakers instead of caretakers? What was he thinking? Did he have a limited audience in view, a spiritually elite caste who can do things the rest of us would be foolish to attempt? Was he speaking metaphorically rather than literally? Did he intend "greater works" as a relative concept, meaning that we'll do greater things with Jesus than we ever imagined, but not things that are truly greater works than his own?

We balk at the idea that he intends to be taken at his word. Taking Jesus literally at this point would turn our worlds upside down. It would be, frankly, dangerous. Even in conservative, evangelical, Bible-preaching churches that insist on fidelity to the infallible Scriptures, we are not prepared to believe the words of the Living Word at this point.

Greater works? Literally? Surely Jesus can't be serious.

His words are hard. They challenge our worldview, experience, and catechetical instruction. So we explain them away. But their clear meaning persists, and we are troubled by it.

For all our objections—intellectual, experiential, theological—a straightforward reading of Jesus is warranted. Occam's razor, a rule in science and philosophy, tells us that the simplest of two or more competing theories is preferable. In this instance, we can either attempt interpretive gymnastics to reduce the force of Jesus' words, or we can accept them at face value. It's simpler to opt for the latter. It's also more consistent with how we interpret Jesus' statements in John 14 up to this point. Consider what he says in the prior eleven verses:

1. Trust God and trust in me (v. 1)
2. I'm going to prepare a place for you in heaven (v. 2)
3. You will be with me after this life (v. 3)
4. I am the only way to the Father (v. 6)
5. If you've seen me and know what I am like then you've seen the Father and know what he is like (v. 9)
6. I don't invent my own things to say or do—I'm doing and saying what the Father wants (vv. 10–11)

Along with the vast majority of biblical commentators, we read Jesus' words in John 14:1–11 plainly and understand them as pointing to actual, not metaphorical, truth. Jesus really is the only way to the Father. He does truly and accurately show us the Father. He calls for absolute trust. These things are true, patently so.

Why, then, are we reluctant to read verse twelve through the same, simple lenses? Here Jesus prophesies extraordinary kingdom expressions—"greater works"—in the lives of ordinary kingdom citizens. He sees no disconnect between what he's been doing and what his most committed followers will be up to. Jesus models the naturally supernatural life that his friends will live because, just as he is in the Father and they are one, so his followers will enjoy the same intimate communion with the Father.

Fellowship is the Foundation

The foundation of our commission to dangerous, supernatural living is the same as for Jesus: fellowship with the Father. This crucial truth, and our willingness to live into the fullness of its implications, compels us into a naturally supernatural life.

Many of us disbelieve our call to supernatural ministry—healing, blessing, raising, delivering—because we can see our temporal lives and limitations, and little else. We've prayed for the sick and nothing happened. Or worse, they got sicker. We've tried casting out a demon or two, and other than leaving us feeling silly and superstitious, not much occurred. Frankly, the results of our attempts at ministry haven't been impressive. We may yearn for something greater, suspect that we were born for something more, but when we look in the mirror an honest report of our reflection is sobering: we're ordinary people whose lives and actions are unremarkable. Healing the sick? Giving life to the poor? Exorcisms? Raising the dead? Pipe dreams. We'd settle for a consistent quiet time and a victory or two over besetting sins. Granted, it's not much, but at least it's attainable.

Given our inherent frailty and track record of unspectacular lives with Christ, is it any wonder we conclude that other-worldly expressions of the kingdom are out of our league? When we look at ourselves honestly, what other conclusion is available to us?

At precisely this point we arrive at a watershed moment: disappointment or destiny. Either can be ours. If we persist in self-preoccupation (under the guise of ruthless honesty), we will ultimately reap disappointment. We cannot engage the dangerous life of following Jesus with our eyes fixed on ourselves. Relentless self-examination is a disabling flaw. We may fall into narcissistic fascination with ourselves when we stare too long into the looking glass, or we may be so discouraged by our liabilities that we rationalize disobedience on the basis of our weaknesses. So Dietrich Bonhoeffer adjures his students at his illegal seminary in Nazi Germany, "The Christian should not be constantly feeling his spiritual pulse."[16] There is no upside to focusing on ourselves.

Jesus' invitation to dangerous living is predicated on eyes that are fixed on the Father and centered in the life of God. Here, in the heart of the Father-Son-Holy Spirit love relationship, disappointment with ourselves is exchanged for the destiny of heaven, what Paul describes as "the prize of the upward call of God in Christ Jesus" (Philippians 3:14 NASB).

The key to becoming the dangerous kind is availing ourselves of the abundant life flowing from the Trinity: God as Father, Son, and Holy Spirit. Initially this may strike us as unlikely, for we tend to relegate the Trinity to an arcane theological concept having little to do with real life. The Godhead remains at arm's length for most of us, a complex, insoluble mystery defying explanation.

In fact, however, it is in the Trinity that the deepest longings of the human heart are realized. "Let God be defined not so much by holiness and sovereignty in which loving relatedness is incidental, but by the dance of trinitarian life," writes Clark Pinnock.[17] Pinnock is not lobbying for diminished appreciation of God's attributes; he is calling us to a deeper encounter with the loveliness of God's Person, for here and only here can real life be found. We are

---

[16] Dietrich Bonhoeffer, *Life Together: The Classic Exploration of Christian Community* (New York: Harper and Row, 1954), 27.

[17] Clark Pinnock, *Flame of Love: A Theology of the Holy Spirit* (Downers Grove, IL: InterVarsity Press, 1996), 47-48.

not invited by Jesus into an abstract, academic investigation of the character and attributes of God, but into an encounter with Truth that will set us free.[18] The Holy Spirit does not guide us to principles; he guides us to a Person. He doesn't guide us to the truth, but to a Person who declares, *"I am the Truth"* (John 14:6). Even the Bible, so often characterized as an instruction manual for Christian living, is more than a collection of Christian principles to live by. It is God's accurate, authoritative standard for how we live with him and others, and when we open the Bible, God purposes to bring us face to face with himself. Not with ideas, concepts, or propositions. With himself.

So we have two options: we can study the truth and learn about it, or we can enter into a relationship with the One who is Truth, and experience it, and embrace the dangerous life that ensues.

We don't become dangerous by committing ourselves to right principles, attending the right church, or reading the right books. We become dangerous by committing ourselves utterly to Jesus and finding life exactly where he did: in fellowship with the Father. If we want to be where the action is we need be found where the action is initiated: in fellowship with the Father, Son, and Holy Spirit.

The triune God exists not as a passionless deity in three persons, each with a job to do, but in vibrant, lavish, unrestrained love. The Father adores the Son: "You are my *beloved Son*, and I am *fully pleased* with you." The Son, in the freedom and fellowship of the Spirit, cries out: "Abba! Father!" The beloved disciple describes Jesus as being "in the bosom of the Father" or as the one "who exists at the very heart of the Father."[19] This is the grammar of love, language of overflowing mutual affection and delight, a divine dance of passionate embracing and life.

When we are in Christ, the Spirit calls us to participate in the divine dance of the Father's abundant love relationship with the

---

[18] See John 8:32.

[19] Mark 1:11 NLT (emphasis added); Mark 14:36 NIV; John 1:18 KJV, MSG.

Son.[20] The bosom of the Father is where Jesus drew his own life and this unparalleled intimacy was the wellspring of Jesus' understanding of his earthly calling and destiny. It is to be ours as well.

Jesus portrayed his friendship with the Father as the motivating factor for his entire ministry. His earliest recorded statement when he was only twelve years old witnesses to this. When his distressed parents finally located him in the Temple, sitting with the religious leaders and discussing deep theological questions, a nonplussed Jesus asked them (Luke 2:49 MSG), "Why were you looking for me? Didn't you know that I had to be here, dealing with the things of my Father?"

Later, after launching his public ministry, he constantly reminded his disciples why he was doing what he was doing. "The Father and I are one," he said (John 10:30 NLT). So deep is our friendship, he told them, that "I have not spoken on My own, but the Father Himself who sent Me has given Me a command as to what I should say and what I should speak" (John 12:49 HCSB). He gives religious officials the same explanation, even though this revelation will only offend them. "I assure you," he tells them, "the Son can do nothing by himself. He does only what he sees the Father doing. Whatever the Father does, the Son also does. For the Father loves the Son and tells him everything he is doing" (John 5:19-20 NLT).

Jesus' ministry springs from the river of love flooding every aspect of the inner life of the triune God. Love compels the Father to share everything with the Son. Love commands the heart of Jesus and directs his obedience. Love inspires the movement and flow of the Spirit. Love is in all and is all, and every expression of Jesus' calling is saturated with its sweetness, strength, and beauty. Little

---

[20] The concept of the inner life of the Trinity as "divine dance" is ancient. As Barbara Blesse notes in an online weekly Scripture reading for The Catholic Theological Union, the imagery "originated with John Damascene and Eastern theology and the term is related to the Greek word *perichoreo*, which signifies cyclical movement. This notion suggests that the relationships within the Trinity resemble a divine dance in which the three 'Relations' (Father/Creator/Parent, Son/Redeemer/Word, Spirit/Life-Giver/Sustainer) 'hold hands' in a joyful expression of unity and love. Each 'Relation' is continuously and consistently, generously and graciously, giving love and receiving love as they dwell within one another" (Barbara Blesse, O.P., "The Solemnity of the Most Holy Trinity," reading for June 3, 2007, http://learn.ctu.edu [accessed April 22, 2009]).

wonder, then, that the catalyst for Jesus' words and works is the Father's pleasure. Pleasing his Abba is his highest motivation, and everything he does is done with an eye toward the Father's pleasure, rather than his own or others'. "I always do what pleases him," Jesus explains to his friends. "I have no desire to do what is pleasing to Myself ... but only the will and pleasure of the Father Who sent Me" (John 8:29b NIV; 5:30 AMP).

The Pleasure Principle

This is among the more remarkable aspects of Jesus' ministry—it is characterized by pleasure. Specifically, the joy he takes in living for the Father's pleasure. So complete is his trust in the Father, so unbounded is his confidence in the Father's love and affection, that Jesus moves and acts in genuine freedom. The Father's pleasure has become his own; his ministry life is fueled not by a sense of obligation for what needs to be done, but an overflow of love for his Abba.

It is a massive departure from the example set by the religious leaders of his time, who worked hard to do the right thing the right way, and carefully policed the behaviors of the rank and file. Their obedience was generated by a profound allegiance to the law and its particularities, and they kept spiritual scorecards based on religious behaviors. Theirs was a grind-it-out life of human efforts to toe the line. It left their hearts hard and opened them to Jesus' searing criticism. "You're hopeless, you religion scholars and Pharisees! Frauds! You're like manicured grave plots, grass clipped and the flowers bright, but six feet down it's all rotting bones and worm-eaten flesh. People look at you and think you're saints, but beneath the skin you're total frauds" (Matthew 23:27-28 MSG).

Is it any wonder that Jesus so completely captured the hearts of the common people, who were worn down by the demands of religious life? Where their leaders moved rigidly out of fealty to the law, Jesus moved freely in the pleasure of the Father. Joy and freedom were Jesus' offspring, life sprang up from within him, and so people clamored to be near him. Jesus was attractive because he walked in the richness of true fellowship with the Father, and he opened the way for anyone desiring the same intimacy and communion with God.

What Jesus offered, then and today, is life. Real life, endless, abundant, and authentic. What Jesus issued, then and now, is an invitation to the divine dance of the Father, Son, and Spirit. The Father's pleasure, not faultless propriety, drives the life worth living. Jesus leads people not into a rule-following purgatory, but into a dream releasing, destiny affirming kingdom life.

The Good Life is not the Easy Life

To be clear, Jesus does not invite us into an easy life. "If you belonged to the world, it would love you as its own. As it is, you do not belong to the world, but I have chosen you out of the world. That is why the world hates you," Jesus told his disciples. "Remember the words I spoke to you: 'No servant is greater than his master.' If they persecuted me, they will persecute you also" (John 15:19-20a NIV).

He told them, "You can enter God's Kingdom only through the narrow gate. The highway to hell is broad, and its gate is wide for the many who choose the easy way" (Matthew 7:13 NLT). The life Jesus offers is not at all easy. His way led to his murder on the cross. If we follow him, we, too, will find a cross waiting for us. "He who does not take up his cross and follow Me {cleave steadfastly to Me, conforming wholly to My example in living and, if need be, in dying also} is not worthy of Me" (Matthew 10:38 AMP).

Jesus invites us into the good life, into an existence drenched with and characterized by the goodness of the Father. However, this does not equate to a life of unending success and personal satisfaction. Jesus' life is replete with betrayal, misunderstanding, character assassination, minimal results, and at its conclusion complete abandonment. For those who follow him he predicts family conflict, fractured friendships, false accusations, costly obedience, and death. But for all that, the life he offers is good, for it is centered in the very heart of God and filled with God's superabundant love and life-giving approval.

In exchanging the religious life for the good life we do not labor for God's approval (which he's already given), nor the approval of others (which is fleeting and conditional). We do not function out of duty or from a sense of obligation like the religious experts in Jesus' day, gritting our teeth and gutting out the requirements of our faith. We do not push ourselves to "perform" ministry, knowing it's expected of us. We do not work hard with our own energy to curb our sinful proclivities. We do not accept the limitations of a highly rationalistic, post-Enlightenment worldview teaching us that to believe in supernatural realities is akin to believing in fairy tales. We do not agree that we are fated to live one-dimensional, unremarkable, ordinary lives.

Instead, receiving it as a lovely gift, we enter the divine dance of the Father, Son, and Holy Spirit. We experience the Father's pleasure and the true happiness of bringing him pleasure, and find our energies refreshed. Even as Jesus found illimitable power in fellowship with the Father, so do we. In fact, we must. There is no other way for us to be dangerous. Short of finding our lives flowing from the divine dance of the Trinity, we will be inclined to look at ourselves—our gifting, training, capacity. If we do this we will believe our success in kingdom endeavors depends on us. But Jesus' complete dependence on the Father frees us from such stupid, shortsighted self-reliance.

The greater works he prophesied for us emerge not from our excellent theologies, skill-sets, and training, but from the life of the Father in us through the indwelling Holy Spirit. We become what we were always meant to be, dangerous people who are potent for the purposes of God in our generation and a threat to the enemy of our souls, as we understand the power of fellowship with the Father.

Jesus declares, "You will know absolutely that I'm in my Father, and you're in me, and I'm in you" (John 14:20 MSG). Here he offers more than a description of his modus operandi. He's giving a prescription for how our future ministry will be shaped. Fellowship with the Father, fueling our passion and directing our words and works, is the foundation of the dangerous life we are appointed to live. This intimacy and friendship with God is the focus of Jesus' great intercessory prayer for us in John 17. He tells his Father, "I am praying not only for these disciples but also for all who will ever believe in me because of their testimony. My prayer for all of them is that they will be one, just as you and I are one, Father—that just as you are in me and I am in you, so they will be in us, and the world will believe you sent me" (John 17:20-21 NLT).

His request for his followers to "be one"[21] is not an expression of his desire that they get along with each other. As significant as unity among brothers and sisters is (see Psalm 133), it is not the object of Jesus' attention here. The unity Jesus has in mind is fellowship with God, the unity that comes from participating in the divine dance of the Godhead. The dangerous life will issue from giving and receiving the love of God, for this is how the world will be shaken from its dark sleep and awakened to the glorious light of eternal life in Jesus Christ.

Being the dangerous kind is both our mission and our identity. We are summoned to the great battle of the ages, to ministry in a perilous time, and we cannot rise to this call apart from the naturally supernatural life of fellowship with God. Only this can lead us away from mundane, tepid Christianity and into the fulfillment of our destiny as followers of the Lion of Judah.

---

[21] As in the KJV.

A Dangerous Kindness

The revolution God is bringing to the church in these days is the move he's always been about: affecting a shift in the atmosphere through an invasion of his kingdom. The ministry of Jesus unleashed an atmospheric shift flowing from his intimacy with the Father. The crowds pressing him on every side loved it; they may not have known what, exactly, they were responding to, but they were irresistibly drawn to him and the things he did and the way he made them feel.

Wherever he showed up, whenever he spoke, whatever he did—he was constantly setting off seismic sensors in the unseen realms. When he preached, demons cried out in defiance. When he healed, devils scrambled for cover. When he released those trapped in bondage to dark powers, evil spirits recoiled in dismay.

It seems all he had to do was make an appearance and entire towns turned upside down, with people rushing to crown him king by force one moment and giving him the bum's rush the next.[22] His every move drew the disapproving scrutiny of the religious elite,

---

[22] See John 6:1-15 (after he fed the 5,000) and Mark 5:1-17 (when he sent a legion of demons into a herd of pigs), respectively.

who pressured him with scriptural puzzlers and tried to trap him with ethical hot potatoes.

It brings to mind an observation attributed to the archbishop of Canterbury: "Everywhere Jesus went he started a riot. Everywhere I go they serve tea."

God's Presence: An Atmospheric Event

The truth of it is, all Jesus had to do was show up. His presence was an atmospheric event, producing shifts in people's experience, perceptions, and understanding. So close and true his friendship with the Father, so saturated with heaven's own fragrance was Jesus, that the kingdom invaded through him.

The key, for Jesus then and us now, is the presence of God. Presence is God's ministry. He doesn't have any other ministry, and everything he does issues from the wellspring of his presence in our faltering, faithless world. The Bible abounds with demonstrations of kingdom breakthrough ensuing from divine presence. Sin infects the garden, and *God shows up* with judgment in hand. Abel offers a pleasing sacrifice and *God shows up* with approval as his mark. The world spins crazily into depthless sin in Noah's day and *God shows up* with justice (all living creatures will drown) and grace (Noah and his family will be spared).

God shows up. His presence releases his power, reveals his heart, renews his creation. His ministry—or to say it non-religiously, the stuff he does for us and through us—is his presence, and those alert to the God-moves and grace rhythms of daily life find, as the psalmist did (Psalm 139:5a, 7 NLT), that "you both precede and follow me. I can never escape from your spirit! I can never get away from your presence!"

Indeed, God shows up. And when he does, his presence is his personal guarantee that, just as Jesus taught us to pray, his kingdom will come and his will shall be done. God strengthens the human heart and breathes courage for noble exploits by the promise and reality of his presence: "I am with you."

- **Jacob receives this promise at Bethel.** "I am with you and will watch over you wherever you go, and I will bring you back to this land. I will not leave you until I have done what I have promised you" (Genesis 28:15).
- **Joseph's dazzling ascendency follows from the abiding presence of the Lord.** "The Lord was with Joseph and he prospered, and he lived in the house of his Egyptian master. The Lord was with him; he showed him kindness and granted him favor in the eyes of the prison warden.... The warden paid no attention to anything under Joseph's care, because the Lord was with Joseph and gave him success in whatever he did (Genesis 39:2, 21, 23).
- **Moses hears these words at the burning bush.** "And God said, 'I will be with you. And this will be the sign to you that it is I who have sent you: When you have brought the people out of Egypt, you will worship God on this mountain'"(Exodus 3:12).
- **Israel's enemies are warned of their looming defeat with these words.** "Raise the war cry, you nations, and be shattered! Listen, all you distant lands. Prepare for battle, and be shattered! Prepare for battle, and be shattered! Devise your strategy, but it will be thwarted; propose your plan, but it will not stand, for God is with us" (Isaiah 8:9–10).
- **Wayward, frightened Israel is reassured by these words.** "So do not fear, for I am with you; do not be dismayed, for I am your God. I will strengthen you and help you; I will uphold you with my righteous right hand" (Isaiah 42:10).
- **Joshua's call and authority are affirmed with this promise** when the mantle of Moses' leadership was placed on his shoulders. "No one will be able to stand up against

you all the days of your life. As I was with Moses, so I will be with you; I will never leave you nor forsake you" (Joshua 1:5).

- **Gideon's call to lead includes these words.** "The Lord answered, 'I will be with you, and you will strike down all the Midianites together'" (Judges 6:16).
- **God's covenant with David reflects this promise.** "I have been with you wherever you have gone, and I have cut off all your enemies from before you. Now I will make your name great, like the names of the greatest men of the earth" (2 Samuel 7:9).
- **Jeremiah's prophetic ministry commences with this promise.** He declares (Jeremiah 1:17, 19), "Do not be afraid of them. They will fight you, but they will fail, for I am with you and I will take care of you. I, the Lord, have spoken!"
- **The remnant's resolve for rebuilding God's house is created with these words.** "Then Haggai, the Lord's messenger, gave this message of the Lord to the people: 'I am with you,' declares the Lord. So the Lord stirred up the spirit of Zerubbabel son of Shealtiel, governor of Judah, and the spirit of Joshua son of Jehozadak, the high priest, and the spirit of the whole remnant of the people. They came and began to work on the house of the Lord Almighty, their God"(Haggai 2:13–14).
- **In the New Testament, messianic hopes were fulfilled in these words.** "The virgin will be with child and will give birth to a son, and they will call him 'Immanuel'— which means, 'God with us'" (Matthew 1:23).
- **Jesus declares this promise to all his followers.** "And surely I am with you always, to the very end of the age" (Matthew 28:20b).

The dangerous kind are dangerous because we, too, carry God's presence. It saturates Jesus' words and works; it is to permeate ours. The effect he had on people, we are to have. When we show up the atmosphere changes because we don't show up alone; we show up overshadowed by the Spirit of the most high God.

What Jesus is doing in the church now is the thing he's always pursued in the lives of his committed friends and followers, initiating atmospheric shift. This shift takes place through ordinary people like us—the dangerous kind—because we have the life of Christ in us. So when we show up brimming and resounding with the overflow of divine presence in us, God shows up. And when God shows up, heaven comes down.

Some may worry about the statement, "When we show up, God shows up." Really? Are we equating ourselves with God? Does this mean everything we do carries the imprimatur of heaven, that all our actions are self-validating and on a par with the Almighty's? Were we to allege such, no claim would be more ludicrous, no self-understanding more specious, no imagining more vain. God is God, and God alone. We are his masterpiece, his greatest work of art, made in his likeness, but we are not God. That job opening has been filled, there's only one qualified applicant, and it's not us.

All the more reason, then, as we plumb the depths of our friendship with God, that our walk with him be characterized by humility and a radical dependence on his Holy Spirit. We know all too well that when we show up, our flesh shows up too. No newsflash there. The truly astonishing thing is this: even though our flesh shows up, so does God. In our weakness his strength finds a platform, in our foolishness his wisdom finds a way, in our earth-bound humanity his supernatural deity finds expression.

He is, as Gerhard Forde aptly describes him, the "down to earth" God.[23] He doesn't extend a ladder from heaven, demanding we make our way up to him. This is the God who comes down to us, first in the person of his son and now in the lives of those

---

[23] Gerhard O. Forde, *Where God Meets Man* (Minneapolis, MN: Augsburg Publishing House, 1972), 18ff.

who have yielded themselves to Jesus, who know him intimately and personally. From our vantage point it's an outrageous strategy, yet God partners happily and effectively with people pockmarked by sin and failure who have thrown themselves on the redeeming mercy of heaven. Consequently, senseless as it is to us, when we show up God shows up, because Christ lives in us and extends his rule and reign through us.

Dangerous stuff, this. But it's God who's taking all the risks, really. He appears content to do so. Our logical, rational objections do not move him. He's aware that it will be baffling to us; nonetheless he takes his greatest risk at Calvary, allowing the avenue of his love to be traversed through the redemptive suffering of his son. "I know very well how foolish the message of the cross sounds to those who are on the road to destruction," Paul admits, but "as the Scriptures say, 'I will destroy human wisdom and discard their most brilliant ideas'" (1 Corinthians 1:18a, 19 NLT).

The down to earth God designed us to be dangerous for his purposes. It's his intention to show up when we do. The world's been serving us tea for too long, and it's time for some rioting to follow in our wake. If indeed we have no other ministry than Jesus', and his ministry brought constant disruption in both the earthly and heavenly realms, then ours ought to affect the same calamitous outcomes. A true theology of the cross of Christ leads us to this conclusion.

If, however, we satisfy ourselves with a theology *about* the cross rather than *of* the cross, we'll end up as spectators of what Jesus did instead of kingdom co-laborers who understand that his work is ours as well. We'll be mere onlookers, not frontline freedom fighters, because we'll be content to analyze the meaning and theology of the cross, examining it like a slide under a microscope, all the while keeping our distance from its real life implications. "You might say," Forde wryly observes, that this kind of approach "treats the cross as though God were merely giving some kind of illustrated lecture about himself."[24] We satisfy ourselves with making a

---

[24] Forde, 33.

personal decision about the cross—and for Jesus himself—without ever being invaded by it. We remain comfortably ensconced in our world while we congratulate ourselves on having come to important conclusions about God's world.

This is, quite literally, a theology *about* the cross. Which is to say, a theology *around* the cross, around its absolute claim on our lives, its complete demands on our hearts and minds and souls. Maneuvering around the cross, we escape the enslavement it brings to the purpose and plan of God. We run no risk of ever becoming bondservants to Christ, captured by his love, captivated by his grace, and controlled by his desires as long as we can keep the cross (and the King who died on it) at arm's length through analysis, historical and textual criticism, and scholarly debate.

This is not an argument against the value of scholarship or intellectual excellence. The Christian community is greatly enhanced when the best and brightest add their gifts to our way of life and understanding. Rather, it is an argument for invasion over and against intellectualized inertia. The invaded life is the available life. It is the Father's heart to touch and heal a wounded world through those who have been invaded by the kingdom life and surrendered to the kingdom claims of his son. To stop short of this is sub-Christianity, a pseudo spirituality masquerading as the real thing but having none of its life, power, or commitment.

When we have been invaded from the inside by the glory and life of God, it manifests itself. It expresses itself. It gets out and causes all manner of calamitous havoc in the spiritual realms.

A Dangerous Kindness to the Forgotten Ones

Jesus calls us to something higher, something, better, something altogether wilder and less tame than our domesticated concept of Christian belief and service. His vision for us is astonishing, daring, improbable: *"I can guarantee this truth: Those who believe in me will do the things that I am doing. They will do even greater things because I am going to the Father"* (John 14:12 GW).

So what does Jesus do? His self-declaration in his hometown synagogue describes the multiple expressions of his earthly calling:

> The Spirit of the Lord is upon me, because he has anointed me to proclaim good news to the poor. He has sent me to proclaim liberty to the captives and recovering of sight to the blind, to set at liberty those who are oppressed, to proclaim the year of the Lord's favor (Luke 4:18-19 ESV).

The first thing he mentions in this dramatic unveiling of his life's purpose is ministry to the poor, those outsiders who stand almost no chance in this life of ever becoming insiders. It is to the inconsolably forgotten that Jesus directs the first declarative promise of his explosive, life-changing kingdom agenda. The poor are the first on the list and the first in line, and we would do well to give careful attention to this reality.

Jesus' ministry is our ministry. The same Holy Spirit who filled and empowered him for his earthly destiny fills and empowers us, and for the same purpose. We, too, have been anointed by the Spirit to proclaim Good News to the poor. Caring for the forgotten is not just another point on the list of our bondservant duties, one of the many things we're to be about in a lost, listing world. It is central to our calling and pivotal in the purposes of God. Exactly why this is so becomes clear as we examine the Scriptures.

We are made for authentic friendship with God. Yet for all those who declare themselves to be friends of God, there remains this acid test: *caring for the poor and needy confirms real relationship with God.*

"He gave justice and help to the poor and needy, and everything went well for him," Jeremiah says of King Josiah, reformer and spiritual trailblazer for Israel. "'Isn't that what it means to know me?' says the Lord" (Jeremiah 22:16). The context for Jeremiah's historical recounting is his prophetic denouncement of King Jehoiakim, whose kingdom will fall because of his shabby treatment of the needy and defenseless—unlike his godly father, Josiah.

Knowing God is everything, and it involves much more than book knowledge or familiarity with the attributes of deity. Knowing God is a whole person event, a reality confirming a divine invasion that entrances the heart and engages the soul. It is the kind of knowing desired by Moses when he cries out, "Now therefore, I pray You, if I have found favor in Your sight, show me now Your way, that I may know You [progressively become more deeply and intimately acquainted with You, perceiving and recognizing and understanding more strongly and clearly] and that I may find favor in Your sight" (Exodus 33:13 AMP).

Knowing about God is one thing. Knowing God personally and experientially is another. Jesus' complaint against Israel's ruling religious authorities is direct and devastating: they knew plenty about God, but they did not have a heart-to-heart connection that would allow them to recognize his son. They had so accustomed themselves to regularized rituals that they could not accommodate radical revelation when it came in the person of Jesus. They would not be the last to make this mistake. Forecasting the Day of Judgment, Jesus describes countless church people who will be stunned to learn that their religious activity was no substitute for real relationship (Matthew 7:22-23 HCSB): "On that day many will say to Me, 'Lord, Lord, didn't we prophesy in Your name, drive out demons in Your name, and do many miracles in Your name?' Then I will announce to them, 'I never knew you! Depart from Me, you lawbreakers!'"

To know God is to love God and to love God is to obey God. And obeying God will embrace this truth: "Those who oppress the poor insult their Maker, but those who are kind to the needy honor him" (Proverbs 14:31 NRSV). Insulting God is a bad strategy in all cases, and it entails more than committing a minor spiritual faux pas. "Insult" indicates bringing shame to God's name and reputation; the Hebrew word, *harap,* means to defy, taunt, and blaspheme.

Insulting the Creator by treating the poor unjustly is the antithesis of honoring God.

Scripture has a great deal to say about the indispensable necessity of honoring God. Consequently, it spells out the unhappy repercussions of failing to do so. Paul is typically blunt on this point. Those who incur the wrath of God share the same defining characteristic: they refuse to honor God (Romans 1:21). In Paul's understanding it's quite simple: honor God and live; don't honor God and die. Why? Because the failure to render esteem to the Lord is at its essence a failure of relationship. "Isn't it true that a son honors his father and a worker his master?" asks the Lord in Malachi 1:6. "So if I'm your Father, where's the honor? If I'm your Master, where's the respect?"

Valuing and loving the down-and-outers is a signal of relationship with the living God because it is an expression of honor and respect. When we esteem God, we value what he values, we love what he loves, we care about (and for) what he cares about. This is why the Lord frames how we treat the marginalized in terms of friendship with him. "Isn't that [caring for the poor] what it means to know me?"

His friends, his sons and daughters, his servants will all be known for this common trait: we waste ourselves on the needy and loveless because that's what God did for us. "While we were still sinners Christ died for us," Paul marvels in Romans 5:8. Or as *The Message* has it, "But God put his love on the line for us by offering his Son in sacrificial death while we were of no use whatever to him." It's no real stretch for followers of Jesus to befriend the friendless or remember the forgotten because that is what we once were ourselves. Once upon a time we were of no use whatever to God. So the world's constant drumbeat to the poor—"You're of no use whatever to anyone"—is no disincentive at all for our personal investment in the lives of the least. We remember what we were without Christ and what we became in him, and we ardently believe the same is possible for those whom society has written off.

Understood from this vantage point, ministry to the unpopular cannot be equated with selfless altruism or the actions of religious do-gooders. It's neither a measure of our personal moral excellence nor our bottomless, bias-free compassion. It is rather a matter of family resemblance and gratitude. We do it because our brother Jesus did it; we do it because all he did he gave to us to pursue as well, in his name. It was in his blood. It's in ours, too. But we do it also because we are mindful of the grace we received though we did not deserve it. We are a glad people and a grateful people who love the last and the least because we're so thankful to the Father for his love for us.

If we do not love and spend ourselves on the poor, we find ourselves fitting the sad description in Romans 1:21 of those destined for God's wrath: ungrateful trivializers of heaven's sweet bounty. Conversely, when we bear the Father's heart to "the least of these" we verify our passionate relationship with him. It is this passionate relationship that unleashes a dangerous kindness that hell will do anything to impede.

It Comes Down to Greatness (Because Greatness Came Down)

Some years ago a national survey asked, "What is the main job of the church?" This question was posed to two demographics: believers who regularly attended church and non-believers who did not.

Not surprisingly, and in line with the Great Commission, Christians identified evangelism as the number one job of the church: persuading those who do not know Jesus to receive him as Lord and Savior.

Unchurched people had a different view of things. They believed the main job of the church is taking care of the poor. If the people who follow Jesus don't do it, who will?

This accords with how Jesus' brother James, the head of the Jerusalem church, viewed the essence of Christianity as lived out between the lines, in real time. "Pure and genuine religion in the sight of God the Father means caring for orphans and widows in their distress," he wrote. And when it did not happen as it should, he was quick with a correction (James 1:27a; 2:5-6a NLT). "Listen to me, dear brothers and sisters. Hasn't God chosen the poor in this world to be rich in faith? Aren't they the ones who will inherit the Kingdom he promised to those who love him? But you dishonor the poor!"

Evangelism and ministry to the poor are interconnected. They do not stand apart from each other, as though one must be chosen to the detriment of the other. Quite the opposite. It's impossible to have one without the other—that is, if we're walking and working out our faith along the Jesus Way.

The Jesus Way is the road less traveled; it is the narrow gate of unfashionable humility and dangerous kindness. It eschews the wide gate of prestige, power, and possessions. The latter route is a broad path to certain destruction and its true north is Lucifer himself.

He was the highest angel but he wanted more. "How you are fallen from heaven, O shining star, son of the morning!" Isaiah says of him. "For you said to yourself, 'I will ascend to heaven and set my throne above God's stars.... I will climb to the highest heavens and be like the Most High'" (Isaiah 14:12-14 NLT). Short of the best seat in the house, nothing could satisfy the lord of darkness. Jesus, the light that shines in the darkness, had the best seat in the house and gave it up to become a servant. The incarnate God came "not to be served, but to serve," and to walk a lonely road weighed down by humanity's gravest sorrows (Mark 10:45; Isaiah 53:3-4).

How easy it is for followers of Jesus to lose sight of this and allow triumphalism to outmuscle tenderness. Even his handpicked disciples, who enjoyed the unprecedented immediacy of his presence and a front row seat to observe him in action, struggled to make the transition from status seeking to sacrificial serving. How they loved to contend for stature and primacy! Who's the greatest? Which topflight performer among them will sit at the left and right hand of Jesus, co-ruling in eternity with unimpeachable authority? All of them felt themselves qualified for the job, but only James and John had a spiritual stage mother lobbying Jesus on behalf of her boys, confident of their credentials for such a destiny.

How little has changed in the ensuing centuries. Their struggle is our struggle. We don't admit it in our small groups or to our church friends, but we long for promotion. Spiritual promotion and public attention. The books we read and the conferences we attend urge us to ascend to the next level with God, to go further up, always higher. And so we forget the seminal truth of the incarnation: Christianity has never been about ascending a spiritual ladder, about going up to the next level with God; it's always been about God descending to us, about God coming down to be with us. The essential movement in the Christian life is downward, not upward. God came down for us. And now we are similarly commissioned: how low will we go to be with those who cannot possibly work their way up to the next level in society's strata? In Christianity, down is the new up.

This confounds our spirit and contradicts our flesh. We're attracted to celebrity; God is attracted to brokenness. We want the headlines; God wants us to care for those on the sidelines. We crave approval and applause; God loves it when we do our best work in secret, where only our Father in heaven sees.

It's About Radical Solidarity

Solidarity with the least, the last, and the lost is the heart of the Father. So it's perfectly sensible that church folk believe the number one job of the church is evangelism. Evangelism—proclamation of the Gospel— is God's personal project of reconciliation with all those who are estranged from him. "God put the world square with himself through the Messiah, giving the world a fresh start by offering forgiveness of sins," Paul remarks, and the result is that "God has given us the task of telling everyone what he is doing" (2 Corinthians 5:19 MSG).

Evangelism, properly understood, is welcoming people home to the only true home they'll ever have. It is standing with wanderers and vagabonds, those who are drifting through the confusing haze of consumerism, religion, and the search for self-understanding. It is walking alongside the heartbroken and the spiritually homeless and affirming the life-giving invitation of heaven: "The Spirit and the bride say, 'Come.' Let anyone who hears this say, 'Come.' Let anyone who is thirsty come. Let anyone who desires drink freely from the water of life" (Revelation 22:17 NLT).

This is the solidarity with the world the Father invites us to enter into. This is what he is doing, and so this is what we must be doing too, for we can only do what we see our Father doing. He is spending himself utterly and indefatigably on those who could never hope to repay his kindness, on those who may never respond to the strong call of love. He is risking rejection and ridicule in pursuit of those whom he made for noble and high purposes. This is true solidarity. Such solidarity with the world, says Karl Barth, "means full commitment to it, unreserved participation in its situation, in the promise given it by creation."[25]

Given God's radical solidarity with the world, it's perfectly sensible, then, for unchurched folk to see the number one job of the church as caring for the poor. Full commitment to the least, the last, and the lost must include caring for not just the spiritually homeless but the literally homeless. Unreserved participation in its situation demands that the simplest acts of kindness—water for the thirsty, food for the hungry, clothing for the naked, shelter for the stranger, visits to the prisoner—must be an innate expression of our following Jesus.[26]

---

[25] Karl Barth, *Church Dogmatics*, IV/3, G. W. Bromiley, trans. (Edinburgh, Scotland: T&T Clark, 1975), 773.

[26] Compare Matthew 25:31-46.

We can frame it as a syllogism. God is for the world. Those in Christ are for everything on God's heart. Therefore, we have no option but to be for the world.

Contrast this understanding with that of the Pharisees, who were separatists. They could not acknowledge any personal responsibility for the wretchedness and ruin of humanity, nor solidarity with those who stood outside the covenant community of Israel. Their deliberate cultivation of an exclusive piety left no room for the disreputable to find a place at the table. Small surprise, then, that Jesus was a constant burr under the saddle of their spiritual sensibilities. He consistently shared table fellowship with charlatans, sharks, and the shuck-and-jivers of his time. Worse, he enjoyed himself doing it. "In reading the Gospels of the Bible," Donald Miller remarks, "I discovered the personality of Christ was such that people who were pagans, cultists, money-mongers, broken, and diseased felt comfortable in his presence." In contrast, Luke reports, "the proud Pharisee stood by himself."[27]

The church cannot afford to affect a pharisaic aloofness. The community of Jesus Christ "does not exist ecstatically or eccentrically with reference to itself, but wholly with reference to *them,* to the world around," Barth observes. "It saves and maintains its own life as it interposes and gives itself for all other human creatures." Or as Mahesh Chavda frames it, "Your job description is to feel what God feels about the world and to *do something about it.*"[28]

It's About the Dangerous Kindness of God

Those relegated to the margins are fundamentally dependent. This is just the way God likes us, and perhaps it is in part why God is so

---

[27] Donald Miller, *Searching for God Knows What* (Nashville: Thomas Nelson, 2004), 123; Luke 18:11.

[28] Barth, *Church Dogmatics,* IV/3, 62 (emphasis added); Mahesh Chavda, *The Hidden Power of Prayer & Fasting* (Shippensburg, PA: Destiny Image, 1998), 68 (emphasis in original).

drawn to the dregs of society. Down-and-outers, dope fiends, and drag queens—who can they turn to? Who will believe the best about them when they are at their worst? They'll never be redeemed in the court of public opinion. All that's left to the hurting and hopeless is the opinion of heaven; they will find redemption in the One who not only loves them, but who genuinely *likes* them, and assures them, "I knew you before I formed you in your mother's womb. Before you were born I set you apart and appointed you" (Jeremiah 1:5 NLT).

The poor—poor in spirit, poor in relationship, poor in hope, poor in life—have a special place in the Father's heart. But the world sees the poor as of little consequence. An example can be found in biblical history and the conquest of Judah. In 597 BC, King Nebuchadnezzar of Babylon captured Jerusalem. He had already despoiled the reigning superpower, the Assyrian Empire, and had beaten back challenges from Egypt. Now he set his sight on Judah, whose king, Zedekiah, had attempted to throw off Babylon's yoke in a calculated rebellion. Nebuchadnezzar besieged Jerusalem, snuffed out the royal gambit for freedom, and won total victory.

History records that "Nebuchadnezzar carried away all the treasures from the Lord's Temple and the royal palace. He stripped away all the gold objects that King Solomon of Israel had placed in the Temple. [He] took all of Jerusalem captive, including all the commanders and the best of the soldiers, craftsmen, and artisans—10,000 in all" (2 Kings 24:13-14 NLT). Nebuchadnezzar did to Judah what the plague of locusts did to Egypt—he devoured everything in his path until there was nothing left in the land.

Nothing, that is, except some people who weren't worth the effort it would have taken to carry them off. "The only ones he left," writes the chronicler of that time, "were the very poor" (2 Kings 24:14 MSG).

Though he completely conquers, Nebuchadnezzar cannot be bothered to take the poor into exile. Why? Because in his estimation they have no value and they pose no threat.

Throughout human history, this has been hell's verdict on the poor and marginalized: they have no value and pose no threat. God counters this with a kingdom-extending strategy that leaves sensible people shaking their heads. Paul explains it this way: "God deliberately chose men and women that the culture overlooks and exploits and abuses, chose these 'nobodies' to expose the hollow pretensions of the 'somebodies'" (1 Corinthians 1:27-27).

This is the dangerous kindness of God: it "gives life to the dead and calls things that are not as though they were" (Romans 4:17 NIV). This is what God is doing right now. And he's doing it through people like us, the dangerous kind, who once were nothing and now have found their destiny in Christ. Through us the Father of Jesus gives life to the dead, countermanding the death curses of hell with words of life and holy calling. Through us he says to those who are nothing in the eyes of the world, who are not even worth the effort it would take to carry off into exile, "Now you are something and someone of inestimable value and noble purpose."

This may be the most dangerous thing we ever do. When by acts of servant kindness and simple love we forge solidarity with the poor and despised, we see the kingdom advance. When by decree and declaration according to the authoritative word of God we call the poor from the margins into the melee, into the pitched kingdom battle for which they have been designed, we see the kingdom advance. Against such the gates of hell cannot prevail.

Raising the least, the last, and the lost from a status of no value to treasured possession is a nightmarish turn of events for the enemy. He has effectively sidelined them; they are not just outcasts, they are the unalive, and they walk among us unseen, undesired, and unneeded. The last thing the enemy wants and what he cannot afford is for the lowly to discover their enduring value in Christ, to move from invisibility to visibility, from death to life, from benign to potent.

This is what makes ministry to the forgotten ones a most dangerous kind of ministry—it takes those who are insignificant and makes them significant. It declares the creative word of God over the lives of the dead and suddenly dry bones begin to dance. It ministers a healing balm to the wounded and waylaid, and sees the warrior spirit within rise up. It takes those who are beaten down and stands them up straight.

This is the power of dangerous kindness and the transforming word of God. Daniel experienced it during an encounter so traumatizing he went weak in the knees, the blood drained from his face, and he fainted. At that precise moment the dangerous kindness of God invades and invigorates. Here's Daniel's first-person account: "And behold, a hand touched me and set me trembling on my hands and knees. And he said to me, 'O Daniel, man greatly loved, understand the words that I speak to you, and stand upright, for now I have been sent to you.' And when he had spoken this word to me, I stood up trembling" (Daniel 10:10-11 ESV).

Is there any higher ministry appointment than this? Heaven's ministrations to Daniel are the ones commended to us by Isaiah: "Strengthen those who have tired hands, and encourage those who have weak knees. Say to those with fearful hearts, 'Be strong, and do not fear, for your God is coming to destroy your enemies. He is coming to save you'" (Isaiah 35:3-4 NLT). The result, from a kingdom perspective, is virtually incalculable, for can anyone or anything be more dangerous than one who is so named by God: desirable, treasured, one greatly loved?

God is building his church, and he isn't building it for us. He is building it to glorify his Son and to reach those who currently reside outside his covenant love. He is building it with and through people who will stand with rich and poor alike. He is building it with the dangerous kindness of unfashionable humility and uncommon love extended by those who once were nothing and now are something.

This must be our witness in a graceless age. "The freedom and courage to love is what the world desperately needs to see in the church and from the church," writes John Piper. "The world does not need to see strident, triumphalistic evangelicals laying claim to their rights. The world needs to see the radical, risk-taking, Christ-exalting sacrifice of humble love that makes us willing to lay down our lives for the good of others."[29]

---

[29] John Piper, *The Future of Justification* (Wheaton, IL: Crossway Books, 2007), 188.

The Spirit and the Mind

As people ordained for a naturally supernatural way of life, but who often find ourselves trapped by the limits of what we are told is rational and reasonable, a sensible question presents itself: "How do we move forward from where we are presently into the life the Lord is calling us?"

An aspect of the answer can be found in Paul's description of Abraham in his letter to the Roman Christians. Reflecting on Abraham's ability to receive the supernatural promises of God he says:

> He didn't tiptoe around God's promises asking cautiously skeptical questions. He plunged into the promise and came up strong, ready for God, sure that God would make good on what he had said Romans 4:20-21 MSG).

The key phrase is "He didn't tiptoe...asking cautiously skeptical questions." Abraham saw the promises of God and grabbed on strong, though circumstances contradicted the very things promised. God's promises defied rational expectations, but Abraham did not allow himself to miss his inheritance on that account.

Everything God pledged to him was impossible and irrational: becoming a father as he approached one hundred and his wife was ninety, a destiny as the father of nations, the whole world being blessed through him. No sane man could have leaned into these assurances, confident of their fulfillment, unless he knew what Abraham knew: that the living God had underwritten these promises with his own character. "I am your shield," God assured him, "your very great reward" (Genesis 15:1 NIV).

So it is with us. God's promises to us and his insistence that we move in concert with his supernatural ways are predicated on his nature, not ours, on his abilities, not our own. Whether or not we join him where he's working depends, as it did with Abraham, on our willingness to move more out of our spirit than our mind. There is no other way to embrace and engage in a naturally supernatural life with Jesus. We must move first out of what God is speaking to our spirit rather than what we can reason with our mind.

This is a counter-intuitive shift, one fundamentally about friendship and freedom. To the degree we deepen our intimacy with Jesus Christ, who calls us his friends (John 15:15), then we will be more capable of hearing his Holy Spirit and receiving what his Spirit would speak into our spirit. The more intimate our friendship with God, the more we will move according to what he's spoken rather than by what we can figure out on our own. And as we deepen intimacy with God there will be freedom. Specifically, freedom to lead and to work and to move the way he has made us. The more we move by His Spirit and the more our lives are conformed to the life of Christ in us, the more freedom we will enjoy.

Many of us have struggled with an endemic bondage so familiar that we have stopped railing against the chains. We live with limited freedom, unable to be who we are, disinclined to allow God to bring out of us what he has put into us. So we settle for what we can get, delighted on those sporadic occasions when something profound and powerful finds expression through us. We were made for noble endeavors but we have lacked the freedom to move unreservedly into that destiny.

As followers of Jesus, whether we have been given a sphere of influence on the international stage or in the neighborhood grocery store, without the requisite freedom to live out our identity and calling we will be less than we are designed to be. We will possess strength and leadership but fail to release it fully. We will be tentative where we should be confident. When this impotency is drawn to our attention, we will likely react unhappily and defensively. "That's unfair and inaccurate," we'll assure ourselves. "I'm not living by half measures. In fact, I've never worked harder to be in alignment with what God has put in front of me."

But objecting on the basis of how hard we've tried will get us nowhere. The issue is freedom, freedom that will lead us into our created purpose, not personal effort. The truth is, we are not free and we don't know why. But if we listen for his voice we will hear the Lord saying, *"I created you to be more and to experience more. Here is the way it is going to happen: you are going to move more out of your spirit than out of your mind."*

The Mind and the Spirit: Primacy and Proportion

In proposing this way forward, the Lord is not placing the mind and the spirit in opposition to each other, as though it were an either-or proposition. We must be clear on this point, particularly in light of the history of Pentecostalism and the rise of the charismatic church in the last one hundred years. While making the way for a beautiful move of God's Spirit that has transformed the lives of countless millions and created an environment for churches to experience both the Word and the power of God, there has existed an attendant weakness among some Spirit-filled believers: an anti-intellectualism and low regard for excellence in biblical scholarship. This unfortunate denigrating of the mind has alienated many in the evangelical community, who have intuited from Pentecostals that embracing the supernatural move of God requires turning off the brain. Such a dichotomy between the intellect and the spirit is both artificial and unhelpful, and it ignores the historical reality that Jesus was an uncommonly bright young man.

Every authentic move of God can withstand the most rigorous investigation; he is neither intimidated nor impressed by the human mind. He created it, intends us to use and develop it, but not to rely on it overmuch. For, as Paul points out, "God deliberately chose things the world considers foolish in order to shame those who think they are wise" (1 Corinthians 1:27 NLT).

The way forward, then, is not in seeing the spirit and the intellect locked in mortal combat (though on occasion we may experience it this way) where only one can emerge the winner, but in understanding the strategic importance of primacy and proportion. Primacy, in the sense of what comes first. To wit: what will be the dominate reality in our lives? From which will we lead first, our mind (according to our capacity to think things through) or our spirit (according to what the Holy Spirit is speaking to us)?

Proportion has to do with how they are mixed, and it's a vital component for those who tend to analyze and overanalyze. We need the proportion to be right so that when the Lord speaks, and we rightly put our mind to consider it, we do not get stuck there. Instead we must allow the Spirit to touch our spirit, and so inform our thinking. Passionate intellect must be married to passionate heart; commitment to the highest level of intellectual discovery must be partnered with a commitment to the highest level of hunger for hearing the Father's voice.

If the problem for some of us is a tendency to rely too heavily on the intellect, the solution isn't that we are supposed to stop thinking. In advance we must disavow the suggestion that thinking is an inferior endeavor, a less spiritually potent response than feeling or experience. Thinking is not optional in the Christian life. We are designed to think. The challenge is that we need to do so in the correct order (first listening to what God is saying to our spirit) and we need to have the mind-spirit proportions correct.

Consider Paul's statement in Romans 8:6. *"The mind of sinful man is death. But the mind controlled by the Spirit is life and peace."* This is the endgame: thinking that is so Holy Spirit saturated that we have what Paul describes elsewhere as the very mind of Christ (1 Corinthians 2:16). When our thinking is controlled by the Holy Spirit, this is the mind of Christ functioning in us. Thinking like Christ, not not-thinking, is what we need to be the dangerous kind. When we think in alignment with the heart of the Father, and according to the revelation of his Holy Spirit in our lives, we are a threat to the kingdom of darkness.

For this to be true of us there has to be a submission of our mind to the mind of Christ. We will not be able to go with the flow of what God is doing if we are constantly analyzing our way through everything. When we are controlled by the Holy Spirit, going with the flow of his life is the most natural thing we can do, engaging both our spirit and our mind, without too-strenuous analysis. What we perceive (through our mind and spirit) our Father doing, we do, for he loves to partner with us for kingdom purposes.

This is the biblically commended approach to our life with Christ. So why don't we do it? What's gumming up the works? For some of us the answer lies here: we have not been trained to live by revelation rather than by reason alone. We have not developed the instinct to think and move supernaturally, to live Spirit-naturally. We are not inclined to move, speak, and think in alignment with heavenly reality. Our culture, our training centers for learning, and even our faith communities have told us the same thing: if you think things through, you can trust your mind. With diligent application of your intellect, careful study, and reasonable input from trustworthy sources, you will come to right conclusions, which will lead to right actions.

How different is the counsel Luke Skywalker receives from Jedi Master Obi Wan Kenobi. In George Lucas's landmark film *Star Wars*, the movie's hero finds himself in the center of the warfare of his age. In the heat and action of that warfare, of course he uses his mind; as fellow X-wing pilots are getting picked off left and right, Skywalker racks his brain for a way to complete his mission without being killed. He feverishly reviews his battle training and is considering what tactics to employ when he hears the voice of his master, soft, penetrating, and authoritative. "Luke, trust your feelings. Use the force. Luke, let go." Skywalker obeys the voice deep in his spirit but he doesn't disengage his rational conscious mind. He still has to fly his X-wing fighter and maneuver it into the appropriate position. Then, only when his spirit communicates with his mind does he know the exact moment to fire his torpedo that will utterly destroy the Death Star.[30]

Like Luke Skywalker, we reside in the great warfare of our age. We, too, are at war. In the heat and action of that warfare, the Father wants us to know that we cannot get it done by thinking alone. Of course we must think, and rigorously. But the human mind is not enough, no matter how agile and brilliant it is. We must be ready to hear and obey our Master's voice, soft and penetrating and authoritative.

The limitations of prodigious brain power is brought into sharp relief when we consider the paradox of Kim Peek, a megasavant whose feats of memory have virtually no equal in human experience. The inspiration for Dustin Hoffman's character in *Rain Man*, Kim Peek remembered every piece of music he ever heard. Like Mozart, he had the rare gift of perfect pitch. He once sat down with a music professor at a university in Utah and in ten minutes had exhausted her entire knowledge database of all the years of her study. His father could not take him to a concert, a symphony, or an opera because Peek knew the complete musical score and if one note was missed or played differently, he stood up and demanded to know why.

Peek read at a superhuman rate and recalled virtually every word. He could read two pages in eight to ten seconds, reading the left page with his left eye and the right page with his right eye. *Simultaneously.* Peek had ninety-eight percent retention; the standard deviation for the rest of us is forty-three percent.

Peek, who died in 2009, also suffered social difficulties, possibly resulting from a developmental disability related to congenital

---

[30] *Star Wars Episode IV: A New Hope*, George Lucas, writer, director (20th Century Fox, 1977).

brain abnormalities. Though deemed a genius in fifteen separate disciplines, he struggled with normal conversation, interpersonal interaction, and became quickly, almost childishly frustrated when others could not understand or did not agree with him. He had a legendary memory capable of recalling the content from the 12,000 books he read, but throughout his life had difficulty with the abstract concepts—like hope, love, and forgiveness—so essential to meaningful relationships.[31] Peek powerfully illustrates that the brute force of a brilliant mind by itself is not enough. For all the knowledge at his disposal, without the Holy Spirit even a megasavant cannot know the deep things of God.

Paul helps us to see the primacy and proportion of the spirit-mind partnership in a letter to his friends in Corinth.

> But it was to us that God revealed these things by his Spirit. For his Spirit searches out everything and shows us God's deep secrets. No one can know a person's thoughts except that person's own spirit, and no one can know God's thoughts except God's own Spirit. And we have received God's Spirit (not the world's spirit), so we can know the wonderful things God has freely given us. When we tell you these things, we do not use words that come from human wisdom. Instead, we speak words given to us by the Spirit, using the Spirit's words to explain spiritual truths. But people who aren't spiritual can't receive these truths from God's Spirit. It all sounds foolish to them and they can't understand it, for only those who are spiritual can understand what the Spirit means (1 Corinthians 2:10-14 NLT).

This is the bottom line. The deep things of God cannot be accessed by intellectual application. The discovery requires the revelatory work of the Holy Spirit. We cannot think our way into the deep and wondrous things of God.

---

[31] "Kim Peak," Wikipedia, http://en.wikipedia.org/wiki/Kim_Peek (accessed February 6, 2010).

No surprise, then, that God regularly uses the foolish and takes special delight deploying them to confound the super-smart. Maybe the reason those with high-functioning intellects are at a disadvantage when it comes to the ways of God is that the wise are harder for him to get a hold of. It is harder to get their attention, because those with beautiful minds tend to think they know something. Quite a few somethings, in fact. As gifted possessors of knowledge, they expect others to come to them for direction and insight. They certainly do not expect to have to go to anyone else for the same.

But when you don't think you know something, when you don't think you know much at all, what do you do? You go to someone else. And who do you go to? If you're paying attention, you go to the One who knows everything because he is the beginning and ending of everything.

Paul draws a distinction between two kinds of people in 1 Corinthians 2:13–14. He describes those who are *pneumatikois,* supernatural and spiritual, and compares them with those who are *psychikos,* soulish and natural. Those who are *pneumatikois* are controlled by and sensitive to the Holy Spirit. In contrast, those who are *psychikos* are subject to the mind, the will, the emotions, and the body. They cannot access or evaluate spiritual realities since these can only be perceived by supernatural revelation. Consequently they rarely escape their own minds, which set the boundaries for what can be known.

This confinement results from sin. Prior to sin's entrance in the Garden, Adam and Eve enjoyed an unpolluted humanity in which God's life entered theirs and directed their minds, wills, emotions, and bodies. From the beginning God designed us to move easily with the rhythms of his gracious presence, his Spirit communicating with our spirit so what we do, what we think, what we say, how we feel emerges from our intimate communion with him. But sin ruined everything. So expertly has it spread its lethal poison that we are continually subject to the demands of the body, mind, will, and emotions, and we think this is the way it has to be.

Until God steps in. Until we hear his voice inviting us to receive eternal life and the restoration of our original design to walk in sweet friendship with him. Suddenly there is a new normal. Before, we were trapped in *koyaanisqatsi,* a life out of balance.[32] Moving more out of our spirit than our mind, we understand that this new way of being is really about friendship and freedom. The more intimate our life with him the more naturally we move out of our spirit, which has been touched and informed by his Holy Spirit. The result is that we are free to be who he made us to be because we are being led by his Holy Spirit, rather than by our emotions, body, or mind.

Who, Not How, Is Our Starting Point

Pragmatists are bound to ask, "Yes, but how do we do it—how do we resolve the tension and make the shift?" It's a good question, and an important one, but it is not the first question we should ask. Rather than worrying about how we change from an over-reliance on rational thought, we must begin with the question of who. Who is this One who's inviting us into a new way of being, moving, and thinking? Who is this One who is redirecting our understanding of what it means to be an authentically spiritual person?

"How?" is the wrong first question because being the dangerous kind is ultimately about relationship, not getting something right. It's about learning that as good as it feels to achieve and accomplish, nothing is more satisfying than him. When we live in this reality we will be at peace, for this is the promise of Scripture: *"The mind controlled by the spirit is life and peace"* (Romans 8:6b NIV).

---

[32] A word from the Hopi language meaning: 1. crazy life; 2. life in turmoil; 3. life disintegrating; 4. life out of balance; and 5. a state of life that calls for another way of living. Compare http://www.philipglass.com/music/recordings/Koyaanisqatsi-09.php (accessed March 2, 2010).

Moving more out of our spirit than out of our mind has to do with relationship, not a methodology or specialized theology. Strange and unlooked for that the key to making the shift (indeed, a key for being the dangerous kind) would not be working out how to do it, but discovering who God is. It is counter intuitive but true that the starting point for this entire shift in us is not *us*. It is rather the grandeur of God. Phillip Yancy draws this to our attention in his book on prayer. "We are, we humans, a mere pinch of dust scattered across the surface of a non-descript planet. At the heart of all reality is God, an unimaginable source of both power and love. In the face of such reality we can grovel in humanoid humility or we can, like the psalmist, look up instead of down, to conclude, 'Oh Lord, our Lord, how majestic is your name in all the earth!'"[33]

This is the starting point: the grandeur, the excellence, the perfection of God. This does not resolve all of our questions, nor obviate the need to ask them. But what it does is beckon us first to dive into the Father's heart, into the reality of who he is. Our thinking will not stop—how impoverished would our experience of this world be!—but perhaps our over-thinking will subside and we will find ourselves more instinctively moving out of God's life rather than our own.

There we will find freedom, which is, after all, what Paul says was the point of the whole thing. "It is for freedom that Christ has set us free!" he writes to the Christ-followers in Galatia (Galatians 5:1 NIV), declaring both their destiny and spiritual inheritance. In freedom and friendship with the One who knew us before the foundations of the world we may become a truly dangerous people, potent for the purposes of God and a threat to the wicked ways of the enemy of our soul.

This is a potentially risky prescription in a culture that has Oprah-ized almost everything, open to the misapprehension that our feelings are nearly infallible navigational tools for the journey we're on. They're not, of course. Feelings, like our thoughts, must be submitted to Christ, measured against the word of his grace

---

[33] Phillip Yancy, *Prayer—Does It Make Any Difference?* (Grand Rapids, MI: Zondervan, 2006), 21.

in Scripture, and sanctified by his Holy Spirit. Still, it can legitimately be proposed that the kingdom life is to be lived in much the
same way the best poetry is written: from the heart. W. H. Auden's
advice to an aspiring sixteen-year-old poet is instructive. "Real poetry originates in the guts and only flowers in the head," he tells
John Cornford, who died five years later in the Spanish Civil War.
"But one is always trying to reverse the process and work one's guts
from one's head."[34] It cannot be done, this working the heart from
the head. Not in poetry and not in our life with Christ. We work
first from the heart, the heart the Lord has given us as pure gift.
Not the stony old heart, the diseased and deceitful heart enslaved
to sin. No, we live from our new heart, a heart of flesh and tenderness, a heart freed to hear and respond to our Abba's voice. This
heart works easily and effortlessly with the mind of Christ in us to
bring us into alignment with the plans and pleasures of the King of
Heaven. That's when the dangerous kind find their courage, their
conviction, their calling. In freedom and friendship the dangerous
kind become unstoppable.

---

[34] Letter of May 4, 1932, quoted in Charles Osborne, *W. H. Auden: The Life of a Poet* (New York: M.
Evans and Company, 1979), 88.

Under the Word

Followers of Jesus throughout the ages have found themselves walking the valley of shadows, hemmed in by life and its dark problems. Anyone who has traversed this territory knows it is unpleasant and uncomfortable and undesirable. When we are stranded in a desolate wasteland, our inclination is to cry out to the Lord with bitterest tears and laments, "This is not good for me!" His response might surprise us.

"You don't know what's good for you."

It is exactly the sort of thing God would say. It's exactly like him to interrupt our complaining with the truth as only he can see it. But he doesn't just see it. He says it, and when he does it is final, absolute, complete.

"You don't know what's good for you."

As much as it pains us to admit it, he's right. When we say "good" we mean "pleasant." When God says it he has our life trajectory in view, the shaping of our character and the refining of our availability for his purposes. The character-forming work we chafe under is often the material he most likes using for advancing the kingdom through us. We can't help wondering, though: would it kill him to mold our character and prepare our life through success, prosperity, and pleasant travels? Why the reliance on the valley of shadows to hammer us into shape?

We'd like God to do things our way. Burger King does; couldn't the Almighty follow suit? The problem is that if God did it our way, it wouldn't kill us, and killing us is what he's after.

What is needful is that the Father's heart for us be fully expressed and his will wholly accomplished in us. Each time the Living Word breaks through, his goal is the same: personal address. Authentic encounter. If the Word does not address us in the reality of our lives, where things are brutish, hard, and cruel, then we fail to allow the Word to be God's Word to and for us. His Word gets relegated to the nonessential category of words we might listen to, or might not, depending on our mood at the moment, words that are alternately interesting, arresting, or unappealing. In the end though, whatever descriptive label we append to them, they are just words. Rather than standing under the Word and its full weight of conviction, grace, and power, we stand over the words we hear and bring our judgment to them. Do they please us? Do they satisfy us? Do they tell us what our itching ears wish to hear? We are prone, after all, to fill up on spiritual junk food and run after catchy opinions that tickle our fancy.[35]

For example, take the typical response of church-goers after sitting through a sermon we do not care for. Not liking the sermon, we conjure up all the reasons—theologically and presentationally—why it fell short of the glory of God. However, nice, polite church folk don't come right out with severe evaluations of the morning message; instead we offer the pious-sounding assessment, "I didn't get much out of the sermon today. It didn't really feed me. It didn't minister to me."

The remark gives the appearance of thoughtful reflection and spiritual depth. With such statements we may fool ourselves and others, but we can never fool God. He who is truth knows its opposite when he hears it and sees it. "I didn't get much out of the

---

[35] See 2 Timothy 4:3 MSG.

sermon today" is us standing in judgment of the words we heard. But when the living Word comes forth, even when it is not handled skillfully or delivered with distinction, it always addresses us, not we it. Evaluating sermons (or the worship set or the building or anything else) is just a technique for dodging the divine Word that exposes our vulgarity, our pride, our vanity. God's Word is the Word that is over us in order that it might be life to us and for us.

The Word of God strips away pretense and posturing. It disarms our arguments and exposes our self-adulation. It doesn't do this sometimes. It does it every time. No exceptions. We have our opinions and perspectives; we live in a culture that trumpets tolerance as an absolute virtue. You have your point of view and I have mine. What works for you is good. What works for me is good. Whether or not it is true, right, and virtuous is less important than a pragmatic embracing of the perspective that all opinions are equal and tolerance is next to godliness. Ironically, God will have none of this. He is, you might say, intolerant of this point of view. All viewpoints are not equal and truth is not relative. There is a Word before which all other words must give way.

"This is not good for me." Human words. Our words on the situation we're in, our take and our talk.

"You don't know what's good for you." God's word over our word, silencing our word. When it's his Word, whether severe and corrective or sweet and comforting, there are no other words to be said. "You don't know what's good for you." God's Word. We can feel the weight of it. It is not offered up for negotiation or appraisal. It just is. No wonder Jesus warns those who follow him, who stand under his Word in all its terrible beauty and authority, "Family. Friends. Reputation. Kiss me hello and you'll kiss them goodbye. My way is the way of the cross."

The Word that stands over us is the same Word that heals us. It breaks what is strong and hard in us that we might have hearts of flesh, being conformed more and more into the likeness of Christ. There can be no circumcision of the heart without cutting, no resurrection to life without first dying. This is what the Word of the

Lord does—it gets us busy dying so it can get us busy living. There is no other way.

Consider again the nature of the preaching event and what God is up to Sunday after Sunday in our churches as the speaker gets up to deliver the message. We've made celebrities out of gifted orators and engaging presenters, hoping that what they bring to the table will be good. We've lost sight of the reality that it's God alone who is good in the preaching event. We're disappointed when our favorite speaker isn't performing because we've lost sight of what the heart of preaching really is. Each time the gospel is preached there is only one goal: personal address. There is only one legitimate outcome: authentic encounter. The Word of Christ, the Word we are ever under, strikes like a hammer and falls like fire across the landscape of our lives whether the preacher is a honey-tongued rhetorician or an amateur gasbag.

The Word that Frees Us Enslaves Us

To be a man or woman under the Word is to be one who has surrendered notions of self-determination and free will. Because seen from one vantage point, those who belong to Jesus, who are "in Christ," are the least free of all people. Paul repeatedly describes himself as a slave or bondservant of the Lord. This does not reflect a failure by Paul to adequately value freedom. Far from it. His letter to the Christ-followers in Galatia eloquently argues for radical liberty in Jesus. Believers there had fallen for a legalistic explanation of how their lives in Christ were to be conducted, with the sad result that they were running a religious obstacle course in order to win God's approval. Strenuous efforts to live moral lives combined with a conviction that it was up to them to make things happen spiritually left them exhausted and confused. Paul's assessment of their predicament leaves little to the imagination. "You crazy Galatians!" he rails. "Did someone put a hex on you?

Have you taken leave of your senses? Are you going to continue this craziness? For only crazy people would think they could complete by their own efforts what was begun by God. For if any kind of rule-keeping had power to create life in us, we would certainly have gotten it by this time. Christ has set us free to live a free life. So take your stand! Never again let anyone put a harness of slavery on you" (Galatians 3:1a, 3a, 21d; 5:1 MSG).

Paul wrote from personal experience; he knew this territory well. He wasn't offering up theology divorced from practice. He had lived a life of bondage to rules and religious expectations. Meeting Christ shattered these shackles. Not only these, but the fetters of Paul's perpetual slavery to sin were removed when he came into the revolutionary freedom of new life in Christ. Yet as Paul unpacked the meaning of his friendship with the One through whom worlds were created, he describes this hard won freedom secured by Christ's life, death, and resurrection as a new form of slavery.

Previously he was a slave to the expectations of elite spiritual teachers who had poured themselves into him. He had been a slave to his human desires and appetites. He had wrestled enslavement in his persistent pursuit of impressing God. Now that he was free from these he entered a new servitude: he became a slave to the Lord of Heaven. We see this as he announces himself to his spiritual son Titus, "Paul, a bondservant of God," and to his beloved friend Philemon as "Paul, a prisoner of Christ Jesus" (Titus 1:1; Philemon 14). Bondservant. Slave. Prisoner. Paul is not a free man; he's a captive to Christ. He is not a man free to do as he pleases when it pleases him to do so. Even his self-appellation as an apostle of Jesus Christ denotes that he is not his own but a man under authority who goes where he's sent and does what he's told.

Paul understands all who follow Christ as exchanging one manner of slavery for another. To his friends in the church at Rome he makes this clear. "Previously you let yourselves be slaves to impurity and lawlessness, which led ever deeper into sin. Now you must give yourselves to be slaves to righteous living so that you will become holy" (Romans 6:19 NLT). As a theologian Paul is without peer. As a propagandist his argument leaves much to be desired. In employing the illustration of slavery, Paul resorts to incendiary, objectionable language. Who wants to be a slave? Who wants to be controlled, owned by another?

No one, that's who.

What we yearn for is freedom. It is built into the human psyche and it is an inalterable feature of the American identity. As immigrants arrive from their far-flung homes abroad, they are greeted in New York harbor by the Statue of Liberty and the memorable lines from Emma Lazarus's sonnet, *The New Colossus*. "Give me your tired, your poor, your huddled masses yearning to breathe free." What we want is to throw off shackles, not merely exchange them for a set by a different manufacturer. "Live free or die," the most famous of state mottos, is the declaration not of New Hampshire only but of the human spirit universally, which rebels at every coercive effort to constrain freedom, restrict personal liberty, and tame self-determinism. Who wants to be a slave? Precisely no one. Our insouciant individualism insists we be free to sail on ships of our own choosing, chase dreams of our own desiring, and follow the bold strokes of our own cartography. We will chart our own course. We will blaze our own path.

Our own.

The very thing Paul says we are not.

"You are not your own," he observes, "You were bought at a price" (1 Corinthians 6:19b-20a NIV). This purchase of our lives by the Lamb's blood paradoxically secures our liberty and confers a new bondage of slavery. God, through the revolution he introduced at Calvary and announced at the empty tomb, bought us. God owns us. We are his now, free from the dictates of this world but bound inalterably to his living Word.

We are, as a result of being in Christ, a people under the Word. Not only are we not our own, we are not on top of things, not in charge of our own destiny, choices, or direction. Turns out we're not on top of anything. Instead, we're under. *Under.* We recoil at the thought of it, for it is the brother of slavery; submission and surrender are its cousins. We no more want to be under than we want to be bondservants. For to be under is to be:

- in a lower position or place than
- beneath the surface of
- less than, smaller than
- inferior to in status or rank
- subject to the authority, rule, or control of
- sowed or planted with, as in "an acre under oats"[36]
- down to defeat, ruin, or death, as in "weaker competition will be forced under"[37]

All of these, as they are affixed to our existence, offend the libertarian in us. We have devoted ourselves in our universities to freethinking; we have committed ourselves in our philosophies to defy established religious precepts; we have subscribed in our politics to the principle of self-rule. And now this: under. It is, frankly, unacceptable. We have categories for how we think of ourselves, and these are not included: beneath, less than, inferior to, subject to, ruled by, down to death.

Yet all of these are true of us who follow Jesus. They are true of us because they were true of him.

- **Jesus embraced being in a lower position or place.** "He set aside the privileges of deity and…became *hu-*

---

[36] *Webster's New World College Dictionary* (Cleveland, OH: Wiley Publishing, Inc.), http://www.your-dictionary.com/under (accessed March 9, 2010).

[37] *Merriam Webster Online Dictionary*, http://www.merriam-webster.com/dictionary/under (accessed March 9, 2010).

man! Having become human, he stayed human. It was an incredibly humbling process" (Philippians 2:7–8 MSG).

- **Jesus was considered less than, smaller than by the people he grew up with.** "'He's only a carpenter's son.'... And they were deeply offended with him. But Jesus said to them, 'No prophet goes unhonored, except in his own country and in his own home'" (Matthew 13:55, 57 PHILLIPS).
- **Jesus refused to contend for status or rank, and if in others' eyes this equated to inferiority, so be it.** "The Son of Man came not be served but to serve others" (Mark 10:45 NLT).
- **Though he was given all authority in heaven and on earth, when it came to the frame-up that led to his execution Jesus allowed himself to be put under the control and rule of government officials.** "He was oppressed and he was afflicted, yet he did not open his mouth; like a lamb that is led to the slaughter and like a sheep that before its shearers is silent, so he did not open his mouth" (Isaiah 53:7 NRSV).
- **The culmination of his public ministry saw Jesus go under, all the way under—down to ruin and death.** "He said, 'It is finished!' His head fell forward, and he died" (John 19:30 PHILLIPS).

To belong to Jesus is to accept that in the exchange of our old way of death for his new way of life, we take on his life in all its unflattering and humiliating expressions. Understandably, we'd rather avoid these unsavory aspects of following him and move directly to the glorious rewards. This option is not offered to us despite our repeated insistence that it is our birthright.

We breeze right past Jesus' darker predictions of what joining up with him will entail. "I have chosen you out of the world," he tells his disciples, "That is why the world hates you. If they persecuted me, they will persecute you" (John 15:19b-20b NIV). The world will hate us, which is bad enough, but it's worse than that:

"I have come to set a man against his father, a daughter against her mother, and a daughter-in-law against her mother-in-law. Your enemies will be in your own household!" If Jesus is to be believed, this is what we can expect from both those who know us and those who do not: they will "revile and persecute you, and say all kinds of evil against you falsely for my sake" (Matthew 10:35-36 NLT; 5:11 NKJV).

To Be Under the Word Is to Be Under the Cross

This is not quite the Hallmark version of Christianity we thought we were signing up for. It brings us back to the archbishop's lament. "Everywhere Jesus went, he started a riot. Everywhere I go, they serve tea." The riotous, conflict-laden impact of Jesus no doubt lies behind his hard warning to his friends. At all times and in all circumstances they are to be prepared for their road to be a cross road. "And He said to all, If any person wills to come after Me, let him deny himself [disown himself, forget, lose sight of himself and his own interests, refuse and give up himself] and take up his cross daily and follow Me [cleave steadfastly to Me, conform wholly to My example in living and, if need be, in dying also]" (Luke 9:23 AMP).

His words lay waste to thoughts of jingoistic triumphalism and trial-free following. To be under the Word is to be under the cross. The cross is the ultimate under. And we who rebel at being under anything other than our own lordship resist this under most of all. For what is the cross but an instrument of torture, humiliation, and death? The cross we carry is more than the burdens we bear from others' reactions to our love for Christ; the cross we carry is the signal of our own defeat and the announcement of our own death. "I die daily!" Paul cries out. We are to follow his lead.

For the dangerous kind, who are to get busy dying so we can get busy living, being under the Word is a risky undertaking. The Word asserts its own reality against the reality we would carve out for ourselves. The Word we are under demands fidelity, calls for faith, and countenances no argument. The Word accomplishes what E. F. Hutton could only dream of: the Word speaks and we listen.[38] The Word commands and we carry out its orders. The Word is our beginning, our end, and all the landscape in between.

We sometimes think that if only God would speak to us then finally we'd have peace. But often when God talks, the Word we find ourselves under is the last one we expect or hope. Peter offers an interesting, disconcerting illustration. Brazen and fearless (some might say pigheaded and clueless), Peter issues bold declarations of Jesus' identity and remarkably insightful assessments of Christ's unsurpassed leadership. Following Jesus' perplexing, troubling teaching in the Bread of Life discourse— "For My flesh is food indeed, and My blood is drink indeed. He who eats My flesh and drinks My blood abides in Me, and I in him...He who eats this bread will live forever"—many of his disciples decided they'd had enough and that he'd gone too far. His copse of true believers thinned to a handful. Seeing this, Jesus asked the twelve, "How about you? Are you ready to call it a day?" It is Peter who volunteers their response, in the form of a penetrating question and an unequivocal declaration.

"Lord, to whom shall we go? You have the words of eternal life. We believe and know that you are the Holy One of God" (John 6:55-56, 58b, 68-69 NKJV, NIV). It's not the only time Peter speaks with revelatory authority. When Jesus queries the twelve concerning who they think him to be, again it's Peter who is spot-on with

---

[38] E. F. Hutton was an investment firm best known in the 1970s and '80s for its memorable advertising tagline, "When E. F. Hutton talks, people listen." The commercials featured folks stopping whatever they were doing when someone would say, "Well, my broker is E. F. Hutton, and he says. . ."

an answer he could not possibly have divined on his own. "You are the Christ," Peter announces, "the Son of the Living God!" Just that quickly, the proverbial cat is out of the theological bag. The identity that Jesus has been so carefully guarding is laid bare. The secret is no longer secret. Not coincidentally, this is a turning point in Jesus' self-disclosure to the disciples. Previously he has communicated in riddles and veiled references. Now he begins to speak clearly of his mission. "From then on," Matthew reports, "Jesus began to tell his disciples plainly that it was necessary for him to go to Jerusalem, and that he would suffer many terrible things at the hands of the elders, the leading priests, and the teachers of religious law. He would be killed, but on the third day he would be raised from the dead" (Matthew 16:21 NLT).

Peter's confident assertion of Jesus' messianic identity is not only a catalyst for greater clarity from his rabbi, it garners him the kind of word that all would thrill to be under: "You are blessed, Simon son of John, because my Father in heaven has revealed this to you. You did not learn this from any human being. Now I say to you that you are Peter (which means 'rock'), and upon this rock I will build my church, and all the powers of hell will not conquer it. And I will give you the keys of the Kingdom of Heaven. Whatever you forbid on earth will be forbidden in heaven, and whatever you permit on earth will be permitted in heaven" (Matthew 16:17-19 NLT).

Has a greater and more powerful statement of destiny and approval ever been spoken by Jesus? Consider his words to Peter:

- **He pronounces Peter blessed.** When we use this word typically we mean that things are going our way and that we are happy. When Jesus speaks it he is not merely describing Peter's fortunate state; he is commanding a blessing as he speaks. Biblically, to be blessed means an experience of prosperity, happiness, and the highest possible good.

- **Jesus says Peter is functioning in revelatory wisdom.** How frequently we wonder if we can truly hear God's voice; we are often unsure how to distinguish our thoughts from what we believe God to be saying. It is a great grace for Peter to be told straight out, "You are hearing the Father! You are accurately discerning His thoughts." Not only does this impart faith for hearing God's voice in the days to come, it affirms an intimacy between the Father and Peter, the same intimacy Jesus has been modeling for his disciples.

- **Jesus gives Peter his true name.** Born Simon Bar-Jonah (Simon, Jonah's Son), from this time on he will carry the name Peter. The naming is of enormous consequence. It's essential that Peter knows his real name, a name that carries the seeds of his destiny, if for no other reason than Satan is the Liar and Accuser, and he will always whisper names for us that shatter hope and defeat destiny. When Jesus reveals Peter's name as Rock, he is establishing a truth stronghold in His friend's mind and spirit that will thwart the enemy's attempts to poison Peter's self-understanding. George MacDonald comments, "A name of the ordinary kind in this world has nothing essential in it. It is but a label by which one man and a scrap of his external history may be known from another man and a scrap of his history....The true name is one which expresses the character, the nature, the meaning of the person who bears it....Who can give a man this, his own name? God alone. For no one but God sees what the man is, or even, seeing what he is, could express in a name-word the sum and harmony of what he sees....God's name for a man must then be the expression...of His own idea of the man."[39]

- **Jesus decrees Peter's destiny.** Peter's life-direction is evident; he is a follower of Jesus. Now he catches a glimpse of how his Lord will use him in building and extending the new covenant community. It is vital that Peter know his

---

[39] George MacDonald, *Unspoken Sermons,* "The New Name." Source: http://www.online-literature.com/george-macdonald/unspoken-sermons/5/ (accessed March 12, 2010).

destiny, for there will come a time when his failure is so total, so overwhelming he will be staggered by it. Describing and declaring Peter's life-calling, Jesus assures him that nothing can disqualify him from pursuing it. Peter may go AWOL for a time and hell itself may amass itself against the son of Jonah, but heaven's purposes will be fulfilled.

- **Jesus describes Peter's authority,** which is essentially heaven's own. The church, and Peter as a leader within it, is commissioned to extend the ministry of Jesus—binding and loosing, forbidding and permitting according to the wisdom and discernment given by the Lord.

Jesus' statements to his leading disciple, the words that Peter is to be under, are enviably kind and encouraging. They reflect the invitation Jesus extends in Matthew, "Walk with me and work with me—watch how I do it. Learn the unforced rhythms of grace. I won't lay anything heavy or ill-fitting on you. Keep company with me and you'll learn to live freely and lightly" (Matthew 11:29-30 MSG). Bruce observes that "the terms in which Jesus speaks of Peter are characteristic—warm, generous, unstinted."[40]

Jesus' words to Peter are words to savor, words to live by.

And yet.

They're not the only words he directs to Peter. These other words are stark, direct, catch-your-heart-in-your-throat words. Not the kind of words any of us want to hear, not from anyone at any time, much less from the Lord of creation. They are words we struggle to imagine coming from the One who describes himself as "gentle and lowly in heart." Yet they are his words, too, and they are words the dangerous kind must be quick to hear and receive.

---

[40] Quoted in A. T. Robertson, *Robertson's Word Pictures in the New Testament*, Matthew 16:17, WORDsearch 9 Bible software, build 9.0.2.125.

The Words We Don't Want to Hear

Shortly after Jesus lauds Peter's revelatory insight and predicts an outstanding kingdom destiny for him, Peter finds himself on the receiving end of a brutally hard word from Jesus. It happens like this.

Describing in greater detail the fate that awaits him, Jesus has begun sharing with the twelve the endgame of his earthly mission. The forecast of the Messiah's death and three-days-hence return to life is a terrifically hard teaching; in fact, Jesus' friends find it impossible grasp, and they struggle to come to terms with it. Peter, for one, is appalled. Drawing Jesus apart from the group, Peter, possessor of revelation from the Father, explains to Jesus how mistaken he is. Of course he's not going to suffer; it is inconceivable that Israel's recalcitrant religious leaders should get the best of Jesus. Certainly Jesus isn't going to die. This is just the sort of talk that can kill the momentum of their nascent messianic movement, and it's the sort of thing that can infect weaker minds, planting seeds of doubt. So Peter the Bold, Peter the Wise, makes it his business to tell Jesus his business. Peter makes a calculated preemptory move to cut off at the pass all such defeatist thinking and phrasing. He will rebuke Jesus because he is determined not to allow anything to compromise their mission and all that they have worked so hard together to achieve.

Imagine his shock when Jesus looks him in the eye and says, "Get behind me, Satan!" *Satan?* Just a few sentences earlier in Matthew's text, Peter is feted as a man of uncommon wisdom and understanding, a man with whom Jesus will partner in establishing his church and extending his kingdom reign on earth. Just a moment ago Jesus was cheering Peter on, championing him as a rare leader among mighty men. And now this. Peter has gone from being a signatory of heaven's revelation to a mouthpiece of the lord of the flies, from a captain in the kingdom to a captive of the Accuser in the space of a few gospel paragraphs. How quickly the tables turn! Still, Jesus is not finished.

"You are an offense to Me," Jesus says, "for you are not mindful of the things of God, but the things of men" (Matthew 16:23

NKJV). It is an astonishing, unprecedented reversal. They are terrifying words—awful, awful words to receive from Jesus—but they
are words Peter must be under, every bit as much as he was to live
under the acclamatory declaration Jesus had offered earlier. They
are hard words and direct, meant to instruct not only Peter but all
who would follow Jesus.

What was Jesus telling him? Not that Peter had literally become Satan, nor that he was housing a horde of evil spirits. Jesus
was telling Peter that he had moved away from God's agenda. How
easy it is to do! Even friends of Jesus who are wholeheartedly part-
nering with him can find themselves working their own agenda and
out of their own wisdom rather than God's. The dangerous kind are
no exception. Like Peter, we can effortlessly transition from God's
perspective to our own, and like Peter we can easily confuse the
two. We can, in our own way, take Jesus aside and explain how
mistaken he is and how much better it will be for everyone if he'll
just take our counsel. We don't mean to move in such stupidity and
arrogance, but, well, it *does* come naturally to us.

The moment we do we become enemies of the purposes of God.
When this happens (and it will), we must be ready to hear and
live under Jesus' blunt correction: "You are in My way [an offense
and a hindrance and a snare to Me]; for you are minding what par-
takes not of the nature and quality of God, but of men" (Matthew
16:23 AMP). It's heartbreaking to learn that what we thought was
acceptable service to God is met with this response from heaven:
you are in my way. But it happens. Not often, we hope and pray,
but it happens. The dangerous kind must not lose sight of this:
if it can happen to Peter, it can happen to us. *It can happen to anyone.* Ministry veterans, seminary professors, seasoned pastors, inter-
nationally famous evangelists, total amateurs—no one is exempt
from unintentionally advancing hell's program in place of heaven's.
Being a people under the Word is the only thing that can save us
when we do.

Ultimately, it's what saves Peter. Peter is a man under the Word. One moment the Word is that which he most wants to hear, the next it is the last thing he'd hope to have spoken to him. In their final conversation, before Jesus ascends to the Father's right hand, Peter is restored to the kingdom partnership he thought he'd squandered. Having denied his best friend when the pressure and the stakes were highest—this despite his brazen assurance to all within earshot that *he* would never take the coward's way out— Peter had gone back to the only thing he knew, the only thing he felt qualified to do: fishing. Jesus meets him on the shore and returns him to his heaven-directed destiny by bringing him back to the thing that matters most: his love relationship with the Lord of creation.

This restorative word is a life preserver to a drowning man. We can only imagine how gratefully Peter received it. Yet in the very next statement, Jesus speaks a grave Word that Peter will also be under: "I tell you the truth, when you were younger you dressed yourself and went where you wanted; but when you are old you will stretch out your hands, and someone else will dress you and lead you where you do not want to go." John, whose account alone records this conversation, comments, "Jesus said this to indicate the kind of death by which Peter would glorify God." Jesus then bound Peter to this prophetic word of execution with the command (John 21:18-19 NIV), "Follow me!"

The dangerous kind are dangerous because they are people under the Word. Whether warm and encouraging or strict and sobering, we submit to it willingly. When we exchanged our old life for his wondrous new life we signed away all rights to speak and live under own words. Our own words make a way for us. His Word makes a way for him.

"Follow me!" Make way for him.

"You are in my way and not in line with God's agenda!" Make way for him.

"Pick up your cross." Make way for him.

Christ-followers must know this: Jesus does not give a hard Word that he did not live under himself. Yes, he told Peter about a death Peter would not want to die, but not before he forecasted his own awful execution. He asks nothing of us, his friends, that he is not willing to embrace himself. He does not require us to follow and obey except that he followed every desire of the Father and learned obedience as a son. He does not insist that we carry our cross except that he was made to carry his own cross first. He does not instruct us to give up everything to embrace this God-life he's offering except that he first gave up everything—all his rightful claims to deity and the attending privileges—to show us the way into that God-life.[41]

Such kindness and identification with us cannot be interpreted through the lens of scholarship, Christological theories, or applied reason. It is a truth that can only be accessed through the door of friendship. He is the door into friendship with God that alters the boundaries of our existence. Friendship and love compel Him to be a man under the Word of the Father. Friendship and love compel us to do the same. We are a people under the Word in all its conviction, correction, and candor because our friend and brother was first under the Word himself. "It was imperative that he should be made like his brothers in nature," the author of Hebrews observes, "if he were to become a High Priest both compassionate and faithful in the things of God, and at the same time able to make atonement for the sins of the people" (Hebrews 2:17 PHILLIPS).

This is mystery of insoluble complexity, that he who is the Word should be under the Word in order to lead us into his Word. Before him, before his mercy and goodness wrecked us for ordinary living, all we knew and spoke were lesser words, an inferior vocabulary designed to promote, protect, and advance our lives. But since the advent of his breakthrough into our darkness and the out-raying of his glory into our lives, we have been given a superior Word. This Word is Jesus, all of his words are life, and they change the grammar of our existence forever. We know his Word because we are designed to hear his voice, and we know that all his words are good. Even when,

---

[41] See John 12:33, Hebrews 5:8, John 19:17, and Philippians 2:6-8, respectively.

as is inarguably the case, the Word is that we are slaves now that we belong to him. Again he shows us the way before he sends us on the way. "He gave up his divine privileges; he took the humble position of a slave and was born as a human being" (Philippians 2:7a NLT).

The dangerous kind are a people under the Word. We attend to all his words. We hear them and gladly align with them, stand under them, and consent to be ruled by them, for they are the way to our heart's true home. His Word beckons, captivates, commands, and calls. When we hear it we come home, echoing the stirring cry in C. S. Lewis's *The Last Battle*: "I have come home at last! This is my real country! I belong here. This is the land I have been looking for all my life though I never knew it 'til now. Come farther up, come further in!"[42]

---

[42] Jewel the Unicorn in C. S. Lewis, *The Last Battle* (New York: Macmillan, 1970), 171.

Hiddenness

Transformation is the life-journey of kingdom people. It is an inexorable, ever-forward metamorphosis from who we were before we knew Jesus to what God made us to be forever—people made in his likeness who increasingly resemble their Lord. Paul had a keen interest in the dynamic of life change wrought by the Holy Spirit, no doubt because his own was so complete and so completely unanticipated. There he was, minding his own business—the business of terrorism against the people of The Way—when Jesus knocked him off his high horse and called him into the low country of servanthood and kingdom slavery. Transformation, as Paul explains it, is the lot of everyone who yields to the relentless love of God. "All of us who are Christians," he writes, "reflect like mirrors the glory of the Lord. We are transfigured by the Spirit of the Lord in ever-increasing splendor into his own image" (2 Corinthians 3:18 PHILLIPS).

The unveiling of Jesus as the life, truth, and only way to the Father is the catalyst for our translation from bankrupt, earth-bound living. This unveiling is paradoxical. It results in Jesus being seen and in us becoming less and less visible. "He must increase, but I must decrease!" announced John to his devoted adherents, setting the course for everyone who would ever follow after Mary's son. This is the paradox: accompanying the unveiling of Jesus there is a veiling of us in the same moment, and therein lays the real glory of transformation: the glory of hiddenness.

The glory of hiddenness safeguards the human heart. It protects the dangerous kind from garnering plaudits for themselves and prompts them to insist all glory be directed to God. This glory, the glory of concealment, is heaven's compassionate covering of us, though it falls short of our hopes for ourselves. We have a different trajectory in mind, and it does not include slipping into the background.

Our Appetite for Applause

Jesus said of the religious show-offs of his time, who wore their spirituality for all to see and applaud, that they've received all the reward they're going to get. Which, on this side of eternity, strikes us as a pretty good deal. Because once it starts, applause becomes addictive. Having received a little, we want a little bit more. And a bit more after that. Soon, more is not enough. Our appetite cannot be sated; we need exponential, not incremental, expressions of approval. We pursue it like greyhounds chasing the illusive mechanical rabbit, going all out but in circles after something that cannot be attained. Our identity and sense of value become enmeshed in the responses of people we do not know and perhaps would not especially care for if we did. Modest skills and a dash of charisma masquerade as spiritual authority and we find to our pleasure that we can work a crowd. What we fail to see is that the crowd is working us. They may adore us, follow us, buy our books, attend our conferences, and memorize our teachings, but in the end they are directing us, not we them. We need their hunger, their excitement, their attendance. We need them. We must have them. They prove us. They validate us. They make us real. Soon enough our mutual weaknesses, needs, and appetites become so thoroughly intermixed we no longer see how far away from reality we are.

It prompts a question. What do we find more attractive, the gifted men and women on stage or the One working through them? We know the right answer, and ninety-nine times out of a hundred we'll offer it up. But the right answer in this instance is not the truest. The right answer is that we should be attracted to God; the truth is we'd sell him out in a heartbeat to follow a mere mortal. We're immediately bedazzled by those who minister skillfully and successfully in the name of God. Surely this one speaks for God, works for God, is an emissary for God. It's just a short walk from here to conflating our worship of God and idolizing the performer who comes in his name. So we'll excuse (not forgive, which implies a discernment too often alien to us) all manner of self-promotion, character flaws, and aberrant teaching because we admire the messengers and crave the high we get in the electric atmosphere of their meetings. And when we are that idealized man or woman, the one to whom others are listening and for whom they are applauding, it seems both just and natural that we should be so received.

Everyday language in the church unwittingly (or perhaps more wittingly than we'd allow) contributes to this star-struck culture of personality and gifting by urging people to spiritual advancement and kingdom promotions. The implicit idea is that those in the public eye are there because God promoted them. Two things, minimally, follow from this. One, if God promoted them we are to praise them. Two, their route is to be our compass. Never mind the corpses littering the shoulder of their highway to Christian celebrity: truth, humility, servanthood, wisdom, love. Never mind, either, that they (and we) have received their reward in full.

Whatever will we do with God's stated preference for invisibility? "For you died when Christ died," Paul writes in Colossians 3:3, "and your real life is now hidden with Christ in God." Though our light is to shine, we ourselves are to be hidden.

Our New Life Is Cryptic

Hiddenness is a favorite theme in Scripture and it appears more popular with God than with humans. What we crave is visibility. We want to be seen, noticed, regarded. Advertising taps into this deep river of the heart; we should be seen in the most desirable car, with the most beautiful people, in the most exclusive clubs, wearing the latest fashions, listening to the hottest bands. What we buy, eat, drive, wear, all of it screams, "Notice me!"

Invisibility runs counter to our gearing. Our orientation is indisputably public. The church, its ministries, and its ministers are not immune. Churches issue press releases, hoping to raise their visibility in the public square. Ministries compete for market share, so Christian periodicals and publications are replete with shout-outs for the latest and hippest cutting edge books, resources, conferences, and presenters. Local church pastors have bought the same losing lottery ticket. We believe higher visibility implies heaven's validation: of us, our theology, our methodology. Those who labor anonymously on the backside of the desert often do so saddled by a sense of failure that they haven't made it out of the shadows onto the center stage. They see those who've ascended to the startling heights of public acclaim and conclude: *that's* what success looks like.

Importing this cultural norm into our kingdom expectation is deadly, disingenuous, and dumb. The push to be seen, to be somebody, to have power and influence—these are alien to the strategy Jesus lays out for His closest friends. "You know how it is in this world," Jesus says, "how leadership is reduced to lordship, how those who are in authority demonstrate it by controlling, manipulating, and punishing those under their thumbs. Well, that's one way to do it. But it's not the way you're going to do it. Lead and go low. Lead and serve. Lead and give preference to the last. Lead and love. Here's the lowdown: leaders take love seriously but they take themselves with a grain of salt. They hold the hurting, rejected, lonely, damaged. They hold more hearts and more hands, not more press conferences."

So the Father tells us, "You died when Christ died and your real life is now hidden with Christ in me." Hidden. Concealed. Guarded. Inextricably set in and covered over. *Krypto*, in the Greek. We get our word cryptic from it, a word that eschews attention, publicity, and obviousness. It speaks of mystery, of something lying beneath the surface, of something we do not see at first glance or even at the second or third. Embedded, too, in this English word is the word for where the dead are placed: the crypt. Those of us who are in Christ have been placed in the crypt. Our old life, the dead, slave-to-sin life, the sell-your-soul-for-public-applause life? That's in the crypt. We've gotten busy dying so we can get busy living. Our new life is cryptic, it's concealed in Christ. Consequently, we know things only dead people know and can go places only dead people can go.

This hiddenness, what does it mean? What are the implications of this divine concealing? It means that when people see us, they see him. The experience for them is puzzling; they have no grid for it. This has long been the way of it. When the religious leaders of Israel interrogated Peter and John, they could not grasp what they were seeing. They could not make sense of these men. They threw up their hands in frustration and could only articulate one conclusion: these men had been with Jesus. Peter and John themselves were nothing, they were nobodies with no education. They were invisible. Cryptic. Hidden. Years later, Peter offered this advice to those who found themselves in the same situation: "Always be ready to give an explanation for the hope that is in you" (1 Peter 3:15). Now, explanations are not required for the patently obvious. No reasons must be proffered for that which is self-evident and clearly seen. Explanations are reserved for mysteries, for that which is concealed and cryptic.

Lost Dogs at the Wigwam Hotel

Against this backdrop of hiddenness consider the Lost Dogs, a critically acclaimed but commercially negligible band in the folk/country underground. Fiercely loyal champions of this relatively unknown quartet occasionally give voice to this lament: "If there were any justice in the world, they'd be selling out stadiums."

But they don't sell out stadiums. They don't play them at all. A recent tour took them along Route 66, where they performed impromptu concerts on street corners, at historical diners and motels, tourist attractions, and campgrounds. Hardly the heady fantasia of American success stories. What band, after all, daydreams about the possibility of playing for thirty people in the parking lot of the Wigwam Hotel in Holbrook, Arizona?

The Lost Dogs have played there, and such luminescent locales as The Cozy Dog Drive-In (Springfield, Illinois), Joy Junction Homeless Shelter (Albuquerque, New Mexico), and the original McDonald's (San Bernardino, California). It brings to mind the old ken: if a tree falls in the forest and no one's around to hear, does it make a sound? If a band plays the parking lot of the Wigwam Hotel and almost no one shows up to take it in, is there still a concert? They play; does their music still touch the stars if no one notices?

The Lost Dogs are a picture of hiddenness and an object lesson for the dangerous kind. Though our culture clamors for front page, above-the-fold notoriety, and though the church has fallen for the same, slick, empty promises of celebrity-ism, maybe the truer thing is this: to be a follower of Jesus is to be a Lost Dog playing the parking lot of the Wigwam Hotel, where a handful of the committed find themselves transported and transformed by something the world neither notices or values.

If we're not careful we'll look at the parking lot and the ragtag group that gathers with us and conclude that what we're doing doesn't amount to much. That it must be *less than,* because if it were significant and successful, wouldn't there be overflow crowds, klieg lights, financial windfall, and tangible expressions of our importance and significance? If we were good and if we had the goods, wouldn't we know it by the response of the appreciative throngs? If what we're about amounted to a hill of beans, would we be playing the parking lot of the Wigwam Hotel?

Jesus was born into poverty to parents living in the shameful shadow of their out of wedlock pregnancy. He was born in the cradle of animal excrement and piss. Had heaven itself not torn open and rained down an angel chorus, even the shepherds (hardly men on anyone's preferred guest list) would have missed his birth altogether. He had a few friends, and they deserted him in his moment of deepest need. For a brief time he drew large crowds and had a robust band of devotees, until his teaching got too hard, too offensive, too cryptic. Then he was down to a handful and even then they were a competitive, hardheaded, faithless band of brothers. When he died, even his Father looked away. For three days he went to hell, which appeared to have the last word.

This is the hiddenness and these are the mean results of playing the parking lot of the Wigwam Hotel. Therein we see a portrait of our transformation from glory to glory.

Promotional Considerations

Not that we like it, or even accept it. We hear "transformed from glory to glory" and we run it through the virulent cultural grid of emerging from obscurity into heightened attention. Most of what we see, hear, and read urges this kind of promotion on us.

What shall we make of this truth, however? Jesus did not traverse the road we imagine most desirable for ourselves. Some believe the road of acclamation and prominence has been appointed for us. Our destiny! Imagine that. But Jesus says to James and John, who wanted the most glorious promotion in all of history, to be seated at the right hand of Jesus and on his left, to co-rule with him in eternity, "Can you drink from my cup?" Clueless, they assure him of their ability and willingness to belly up to the bar and imbibe. "You'll drink it, alright," Jesus replies, "but you have no idea what you're in for."[43]

This is how things stand for those of us who genuinely but ignorantly expect kingdom life to yield promotion and advancement. We will surely advance. We will be promoted. Our imaginations craft countless rewarding scenarios. We've made our plans. But as the ancient proverb predicts, it's the Lord who will direct our steps. And we have no idea what we're in for.

Bonhoeffer puts the knife into the heart of our fantasies. "God hates visionary dreaming; it makes the dreamer proud and pretentious. The man who fashions a visionary ideal of [his life] demands that it be realized by God, by others, and by himself. He enters the community of Christians with his demands, sets up his own law, and judges…accordingly."[44] Our refusal to embrace hiddenness is pernicious, our expectation of public promotion is death-dealing, and Bonhoeffer helps us see why this is so. Once we've seized upon a scenario of our advancement, we insist it be realized. It seldom is. When it's not, the demands we've placed on ourselves, others, and God to make it come true become an accusation against the very life of God in us and against those whom God has provided to walk this road with us.

Our thinking is darkened. Our hearts are redolent with judgment. Disappointment colors each failure to meet our goal of glorious transformation, our promotion into higher and better things for God. Hiddenness? That's for losers, for the mediocre, for those who've failed to impact the world in any substantive way, for those who were never going to rise to the top anyway.

The mystery of hiddenness has nothing to do with rising to the top, but with descending the depths. It has to do with serving, sacrificing, and sublimating, not with conquering, controlling, or

---

[43] Compare Matthew 20:20-23.

[44] Bonhoeffer, *Life Together*, 27.

captivating. It has to do with the altogether serious business of dying so we can get busy living. Hiddenness is the sure and certain declaration that after years of grabbing for the golden ring, "It is no longer I who live, but Christ who lives in me" (Galatians 2:20).

Hiddenness so comprehends real transformation—the glory of Christ living in us—it refuses to be lured into the arena of public notoriety. It knows that every opportunity to talk is a chance to speak of Jesus. Therefore, every chance to advertise ourselves ("If you've got it," Suzanne Somers advised, "bump it with a trumpet!") will be converted into a celebration of Christ instead. Hiddenness knows that even when the work of God through us captures the public's attention, it's always for the praise of his glory. It's not heaven's affirmation that we've finally arrived and are now being rewarded with the success and applause spiritual performers like us so richly deserve. No, hiddenness never gets tricked into that false vision of greatness. Hiddenness knows what we deserve is wrath but what we got was Christ. So how can it be about anything but him?

Why Not Enjoy Your Obscurity?

When the Alliance of Renewal Churches[45] was in its infancy, having been launched amid no fanfare but out of the hearts of those who saw the potential for a network based on kingdom friendships, a church growth expert caught wind of it. In one of his numerous publications he noted the special distinction, not of a charismatic consortium of churches (these are common enough), but of a *Lutheran* network of Spirit-filled churches. This was noteworthy, according to the ecclesiological specialist. Then a major Christian magazine approached the movement's founder about interviewing him concerning the ARC. Would he consent to a published conversation about what God was doing in and among the members

---

[45] A small network of churches and individuals sharing a Lutheran theological heritage, founded in 2002.

of the ARC? When he sought the counsel of trusted friends, this was their wise recommendation: "Why not enjoy your obscurity?"

"Why not enjoy your obscurity?" aligns with a biblical, Christological understanding of hiddenness. And the truth is, acclaim is not all it purports to be. A higher profile comes with companion pressure to live a less than true life, to live in line with the expectations placed on you by the masses rather than out of the revelation of the Father's heart. The instinct to conform to the world's demands once it has you in its sights is hard to disobey. Applause demands more applause, which creates cravings for approval that must be satisfied. Rather than satisfaction in hiddenness, where our rest and protection and transformation and provision are, we stumble beyond God's rest into the world's activity. We tell ourselves if only we can succeed, measure up, and perform according to its standards, then we'll be content. But it's not possible. Each successive accomplishment presses us to further performance. Arriving at the place we had our eye on, we find a mirage and set off for the next thing that is supposed to give us life or meaning or reward.

This is true in the workaday world and in the world of kingdom ministry as well. We are as adept as any Wall Street trader at getting caught like a hamster on a wheel, going, going, going, but never truly arriving anywhere. Not only the things we fail to achieve but also the things we do succeed at drag us further under the riptide of performance. "How much money is enough?" was the question put to millionaire oil magnate John D. Rockefeller. "Just a little bit more," was his famous reply.

When it comes to our accomplishments, who can tell us what "enough" is? How many people attend your church? How many have you personally led to Jesus? How many have you discipled? How many books have you read? How many verses have you memorized? How often and how long do you pray? How much victory have you achieved over sin; how many of the besetting ones have you left behind? How much faith do you have for healing and how many have you seen healed as a result of your prayers? How many prophecies or words of knowledge have you given? How many have you received? Has God's prosperity visited your life? If so, how much of it? Have you matured enough, believed enough, achieved enough for the kingdom of God?

Enough? Who can say how much that is?

Hiddenness is not just a theological construct whose purpose is to keep us from seeking for ourselves that which is rightly and expressly for the praise of his glory. That's a piece of it. An important one. But just a piece.

Hiddenness is God's gracious provision that creates space for us to rest in him. It safeguards us from the life-depleting pursuit of optimum performance, from selling out to something that can only weary, not feed, our soul. Hiddenness is his kind gift. It is life, whole and holy and wholly unbidden to the clamorous demands of our culture. Hiddenness: we think he's putting us in our place. In reality, he's putting us in his place of rest.

The Dangerous Kind and Hiddenness

Hiddenness is a key attribute of the dangerous kind. One of the things that makes followers of Jesus legitimately dangerous is their utter lack of interest in being promoted, publicized, packaged, or pimped. Those who want or need these things can be easily commanded by them. "What *might* I do to get to the next level?" becomes "What *must* I do?" without conscious thought, and soon what we do, say, and think is controlled by what we must do to reach the higher ground.

The dangerous kind do not gravitate toward such pursuits. Not because we are immune to the lure of applause, the appeal of elevated stature, the seduction of flattery, or the thirst for approval. All these things feed and stir our flesh, which, once it gets a taste, demands ceaselessly and pitilessly, "More!" The dangerous kind want to be liked, the same as anyone else. This is true for us and will ever be so.

But while it is a true thing, it is not the truest thing about the dangerous kind. The highest reality and ruling appetite for the dangerous kind is their hunger for God and an issuing passion that in their day and through their lives the kingdom will be expressed and extended. Consequently, credit is viewed through a different lens. The world wants to know, "Who gets the credit?" The dangerous kind choose to say with the apostle Paul, "For my part, I am going to boast about nothing but the Cross of our Master, Jesus Christ. Because of that Cross, I have been crucified in relation to the world, set free from the stifling atmosphere of pleasing others and fitting into the little patterns that they dictate" (Galatians 6:14 MSG).

My Paper-Pushing Dad: A Parable

My dad worked for a diminutive Frenchman whose name was Henri. I never fully understood what Dad did for the international electronics giant that employed him for twenty-five years, and I suppose a fourteen-year-old will rarely have ready categories for wafer production, five-year forecasting, and negotiations with foreign governments for materials and new factories. These are the things my dad did for his company and more specifically for his boss, Henri. Dad gave years supporting Henri's career—writing his speeches, designing his presentations, watching his back. Henri no doubt had his own unique contributions but from where I sat he was walking away with the plaudits while leaving the plowing to my old man.

"Dad," I'd ask, vexed on his behalf (someone needed to be; Lord knows he was unperturbed by the injustices I perceived), "do they know when Henri's giving those speeches that they're your words coming out of his mouth?" Dad patiently explained that the purpose was to get the idea across, expressed well and clearly and articulately, so the company could prosper. Dad was a company man and he knew a native French speaker with good but not excellent command of English needed a particular kind of support. My father was satisfied with this arrangement. I was irked. Frosted. Could no one see the obvious as I could? Dad was doing all the work and getting none of the credit. It was wrong and I wasn't going to stand for it. I let him know he shouldn't either, but he evidenced no conversion to my perspective. I was disturbed. He was unaffected. I didn't get it.

Henri once dropped by our house to pick up something from my father, no doubt another brilliant speech that would accelerate his success and leave my old man in the shadows. He pulled up in a Cadillac Seville. Deep maroon with a cream top. Gorgeous. I took an instant dislike to Henri. After all, he was driving my dad's Cadillac, the car that should have been his and would have been his, if credit were given where credit was due. I stood in the driveway, resenting that Cadillac, despising Henri for using my dad, and wondering how Dad could just stand by and let it happen. What was wrong with him, anyway? Credit—the need for it, the withholding of it, the power of it—had become an accusation against Henri, against the company, against my dad, against God.

Henri came out of the house while I was standing in the driveway looking at his ride, fantasizing a few well-placed key scratches on that cherry paint job. Just thinking about it improved my mood. He saw me staring at the car. "Ees a nice car, eh?" he offered conversationally. I nodded vaguely, noncommittal, unmoved. As he opened the door to get in, he turned to me. "Your father," he said, "ees the smartest man I know. He makes me better than I really am." It was the only time I ever heard Henri speak.

The dangerous kind know that credit as the world accounts it is a fickle mistress. They know that real and lasting credit accrues in heaven when they give themselves to the only real thing there is. They know, as my father did, that what matters is that the message is declared well and clearly and articulately, and that the kingdom of God prospers as it advances in love and kindness. What matters least of all is who gets the credit, humanly speaking. The spotlight is not the goal. The goal is to spend ourselves joyfully and fruitfully on the kingdom, happiest when the Lord is front and center because people are discovering him to be the kindest Person they've ever met. We love to remain hidden as long as he can be seen, and we love to walk with others so that they become better with him than they ever could be alone.

Farmer Hoggett's Affirmation

The dangerous kind love hiddenness. They delight in it as one of God's secret strategies, but not out of false modesty or self-deprecation. Hiddenness is an expression of humility, rightly understood not as thinking less well of ourselves or more highly of others than is warranted, but as a reflection of stability and security. Stable and secure in who God called and made them to be, the dangerous kind don't position themselves for maximum visibility because they prefer that Christ be seen in all and over all. They don't exhaust themselves ensuring they receive proper credit where credit is due because it does not matter. It does not have a hold on them because its illusory endorsement is so vapid and feeble compared to the surpassing greatness of the Son of Man.

This is not religious rhapsodizing, an idealized sentimentalizing of a selfless spiritual platitude. It is not something we say because we are expected to but haven't quite gotten there in our hearts yet. We who are hidden have grown to cherish our anonymity and invisibility—after all, who is Paul, who is Apollos?—because it has come to us as true gift, a grace wind blowing over the burned-out, frenzied plains of human endeavor and calling us to our hearts' true home to rest, to play, and engage in the great warfare of our age.

From time to time we lose our way. We hanker for recognition, we yearn for promotion. It is not enough to be significant; we want someone to see it and speak it for what it is. We may not need the lead role or all the best lines in the play, but we wouldn't mind taking a bow now and again. A few curtain calls would be nice. Not every time and not necessarily a standing ovation. Just enough to let us know we're alive and that someone somewhere is cheering us on, saying, "Well done."

Or as Farmer Hoggett says at the end of *Babe*: "That'll do, Pig, that'll do."[46]

Not even the dangerous kind are immune to the seduction. And in our moments of vulnerability we assure ourselves: just a taste. Not a whole meal, perhaps not even an appetizer. A taste, that's all, of visibility, promotion, advancement, credit. All we want is a spoonful or two of the elixir of applause. That's not so bad, is it?

In fact it is potentially fatal. It kills life, smothers it with the pillow of human affections and longings. No one can serve two masters. In the end one of them must do away with the other. Hiddenness and promotion cannot peacefully coexist. So the apostle Paul, who loved attention as much as any man ever to minister the gospel, arrived at this conclusion: "The very credentials these people are waving around as something special, I'm tearing up and throwing out with the trash—along with everything else I used to take credit for. And why? Because of Christ. Yes, all the things I once thought were so important are gone from my life. Compared to the high privilege of knowing Christ Jesus as my Master, firsthand, everything I once thought I had going for me is insignificant—dog dung. I've dumped it all in the trash so that I could embrace Christ and be embraced by him" (Philippians 3:7-9a MSG).

This is the thing about the dangerous kind: like anyone else they can succumb to the dream sleep of success. They can fall into a trance and trade sleepwalking for walking in the Spirit. But the dangerous kind always wake up. The dangerous kind eventually come to their senses, embracing the transformation from human glory to heaven's, from the need for promotion to the beauty of

---

[46] *Babe*, Chris Noonan, director. Adapted from the novel *Babe: The Gallant Pig* by Dick King-Smith (Universal Studios, 1995).

hiddenness, from clamoring for attention to resting in friendship with him. At the end of the movie of their lives, there's only one thing the dangerous kind want to be told, and only one Farmer's voice that can speak words of life and affection: "That'll do, Pig, that'll do." For the dangerous kind, the Father's "Well done!" is the only applause safe to receive, the only acclaim never to lose its power.

Love: God's Gold Standard

What's love got to do with it? Tina Turner sang this question to the top of the charts in September of 1984. She was forty-five years old and it had been twenty-four years since her last number one single. In those intervening years her marriage to Ike Turner, well-chronicled for its catalog of abuses and barbarities, had collapsed. Ms. Turner had tasted the fruit of success and almost choked at the table of human cruelty. If any singer had earned the right to ask the question and arrive at the answer by personal experience, she certainly had.

What's love got to do with it?

Only everything.

Jesus was once pressed by a legal scholar to telescope the laws of Moses into one all-important principle, to reduce it to its most irreducible core. It was not the first time this weighty question had been posed to a renowned religious authority. Shabbos 31a in the Babylonian Talmud tells of a pagan who approached Rabbi Hillel and asked the great teacher to summarize the Law while standing on one leg. The rabbi replied: "Keep this commandment: 'Do not do to your neighbor what you would not like to have done to yourself.' This is the basic principle of the Law. All the rest is a commentary on it. Now go and study it."[47] The rabbi, believed to be a contemporary of Herod the Great, Caesar Augustus, and Jesus Christ, testifies that the law of Moses—all 613 commandments of the Torah—comes down to this: treat your neighbor in the manner you'd like to be treated, with charity. Love.

Jesus' response to the Pharisee is an echo and expansion of Rabbi Hillel's. "'You must love the Lord your God with all your heart, all your soul, and all your mind.' This is the first and greatest commandment. A second is equally important: 'Love your neighbor as yourself.' The entire law and all the demands of the prophets are based on these two commandments" (Matthew 22:37-40 NLT).

These esteemed rabbis agree. What's love got to do with it? Only everything.

Paul builds on this in 1 Corinthians 13. A chapter made popular by its inclusion in countless wedding ceremonies, 1 Corinthians 13 is a revolutionary battle cry for the indisputable supremacy of love. Though sometimes denuded of its vitality by a sentimental reading, this chapter is one of the more astonishing in all the New Testament for the way it rejects the world's system in favor of God's solution, for the manner in which it decries religious performance and declares love's necessity. Love is Christianity's irreducible core. Paul's declarations are elegant and absolute:

- the highest language of mortals and angels is clangorous flattery without love;
- secret knowledge, supernatural faith, and kindness to the poor amount to nothing without love;
- at the end of all things, three realities will endure: faith, hope, and love, and the greatest of them is love.

---

[47] "Torah through Time," Story Tour, http://projectshalom2.org/StoryTour/?p=117 (accessed February 20, 2011).

While mentoring his unruly, unpredictable band of disciples, Jesus insisted that one thing always be predictable with them and one thing ever rule them: love. "Love one another. Just as I have loved you, you must also love one another. By this all people will know that you are My disciples, if you have love for one another" (John 13:34-35 HCSB).

Love Is the Gold Standard

Love is the gold standard. It verifies our friendship with God and our enrollment in the school of the Spirit. It makes our words more than just words and our principles more than just good theology.

But the unhappy truth is that while love is unquestionably God's standard, it is too rarely our standard. "Christians, on the whole are not known for their outrageous love," author and pastor Greg Boyd comments. "They're known for their intolerance, for their hypocrisy, their superiority, their hunger for political power, and their desire to control society. But they're not usually known for their outrageous love. That's not usually the first thing out of people's mouths: 'What do you think about these Christians, these born-again Christians?' 'Oh, they love outrageously! They don't judge, they just serve.'"[48] If what Jesus says is to be trusted and it really does come down to love, then how can it be that the reputation of many modern day followers of Jesus is so sullied? If Boyd's assessment of how the world sees us is correct, what does it mean for the church?

It means, minimally, that we have settled for theology when what God has for us is life. We have allowed, for example, the Sermon on the Mount to be mere spiritual aphorisms instead of practical instruction for living a life of love. When Jesus teaches about being salt and light, completing God's law, the truth about

---

[48] From the documentary *Furious Love*, written and directed by Darren Wilson (Wanderlust Productions, 2010).

murder, adultery, divorce, and empty promises, he's not putting forward a series of lecture notes for future generations of ethicists to mull over. Jesus doesn't intend to author a classroom textbook; he purposes to obliterate our shabby, selfish way of engaging the day and the world outside our front door. "You're familiar with the old written law, 'Love your friend,' and its unwritten companion, 'Hate your enemy,'" Jesus states, "I'm challenging that. I'm telling you to love your enemies. Let them bring out the best in you, not the worst" (Matthew 5:43-44a MSG).

It's a bracing command, one that presents enormous problems for our flesh-based living. Unless. Unless we manage to limit its intrusiveness by converting it to verbiage for wall plaques, coffee mugs, and greeting cards. If we can render his marching orders for the dangerous kind as mere words—compelling, stately, intriguing though they may be—then we can consider them at our leisure and apply them as it suits us. If we do not cordon them off in some way, however, and if we choose to be people under his word, then his words will ruin us.

They will decimate the decades of living for ourselves, of existing in accord with our personal sense of justice and responsibility. Local municipalities and law enforcement agencies do not permit us to drive as fast as we'd like just because we have the car (and possibly the skills) to pull it off. Why do we imagine God would allow us to? Jesus stands in front of us as we are getting ready to go racing in the streets with our breakneck, self-consumed lives and shuts us down cold. Who is he to do such a thing? He's the Law. Or better, the fulfillment of the Law, and he's bringing a new one that is to govern our lives. "A new command—a forever law that will never go off the books—I give you: love one another." He's talking about more than behaving well, being civil, playing nice. He's insisting that love drive every decision, shape every action, characterize every thought, and influence every outcome. He does not offer exclusionary clauses for when we are dealing with irritating, ungrateful people or difficult, unfair circumstances. The new law is love and it is not written in disappearing ink. It is written, permanently, on hearts of flesh.[49]

Love is a wrecking ball crashing into the artifices we've erected to wall ourselves off from others, especially those we do not approve of. It does not permit isolation to go unchallenged, does not agree that cutting ourselves off from our neighbors, family, co-workers, and planetary co-inhabitants is a choice we are free to make. Love demands interaction and engagement, moving out of the safe harbor of our carefully guarded retreat and exposing ourselves to the pain and hopes and joys of those around us. Love is investment, personal and persistent, in the life of another, investment in someone other than ourselves. Our approach, typically, is divestment and detachment, moving fast and far away from those who would make demands on our time, our finances, our hearts.

The religion expert's question (Luke 10:29), "Who is my neighbor?" is a dodge to keep the unwanted and unwashed at arm's length. We don't care to spend or soil ourselves on those who do not deserve it (as we adjudicate such matters), conveniently forgetting that this is the very thing God did for us. He spent himself, lavishly and gladly, on us. He got down and dirty with down-and-outers like us. And were we grateful? Not especially. Were we deserving? Not hardly.

If we were truthful we'd admit that we resent the implication that we need any saving in the first place. True, we're not perfect but we're not that bad, either, and any all-knowing deity worth his or her salt would appreciate the efforts we've made and respect that we're nowhere near as bad as we could be, and certainly nowhere near as rotten as other people. The more we think about it the better we feel about ourselves in comparison to *those other people.*

If during an Easter morning worship service we were to give voice to our secret convictions, the litany might run something like this...

PASTOR: *People of God, you have come seeking Christ, the Son of the living God.*

---

[49] Compare Ezekiel 11:19.

PEOPLE: **We have come because our spouses made us come.**

PASTOR: *Do not be afraid, for He is risen from the dead. He has broken the tomb wide open. He has come back to life and is living together with us right here, right now.*

PEOPLE: **He seems to have gone to a lot of trouble for nothing.**

PASTOR: *There is no need for your guilt, for He has taken it with Him to the cross and has paid the ultimate price for your sin. This is good news: He is alive! He is alive, and so we can be alive.*

PEOPLE: **Guilt? What guilt? What are you trying to imply?**

PASTOR: *He has risen!*

PEOPLE: **Who? I don't get it. I'm never coming to one of these services again.**

God's love is God's revelation of our true condition. *We* are those other people who cannot be redeemed and restored any other way than love. Whether we recognize or agree with God's assessment is laughably unimportant. God does not need our agreement to confirm the accuracy of his diagnosis, nor as motivation to act on our behalf. Are we ungrateful? Undeserving? Indifferent? It doesn't matter. Love is never predicated on the response of those it spends itself on. Love does not react. It acts. Which is why it's the most natural thing in the world for God to act toward us as he does in supra-abundant love; it's who he is. To do less or other would be untrue to his nature. We may or may not receive him and the new life he offers, but this will not affect his unflagging pursuit of us. His love—true love—is not conditioned by our response. Love's consistency and trustworthiness does not depend on anything we do or say. He loves because of who he is, not because of who we are. Independent of our reaction he has sovereignly predetermined to love us no matter what. Nothing we do or say can persuade him otherwise.

Inside Out

When his love gets inside of us it must also get out of us. Love cannot be domesticated. It cannot be tamed. It cannot be trained to sit, stay, or play dead. It must be expressed; it has to find a way out, and true love *always* finds a way. When it does and we let love flow from us to others, it looks remarkably like God. Or one might say, when love gets out of us and spills over a wounded world, we look remarkably like our Father. This is as we would expect, for we are not loving others from our own resources but his.

Scripture gives us the straight story: we love because he first loved us (1 John 4:19). On the face of it, it is a statement easily disputed. To wit: plenty of atheists, agnostics, and non-Christians have loved without ever having engaged the love of God. Many have loved every bit as selflessly and sacrificially as Christians, and plenty of them have done a better job of loving than those who know Jesus. Though committed friends of the High King of heaven might be expected to know love and do love better than anyone else, it doesn't work out that way. Gandhi had the highest regard for Jesus Christ but he was no Christian. Yet his non-violent resistance to tyranny transformed an entire nation and was one of the twentieth century's most loving movements. Gandhi's life was an elegant testimony to the power of love to bring out the best of us rather than the worst as we interact with our enemies. Meanwhile in Nazi Germany jack-booted thugs co-opted the God of the Bible for their own war-making, blood-bathed agenda, and countless churchmen capitulated without a whimper. Some pastors gave their enthusiastic endorsement and actively joined themselves to the Aryan goals of Hitler's government.

Gandhi and Nazi Germany's diseased national church are obvious historical examples to call into evidence against the principle that we love because God first loved us. But one need not reach back into history to argue against the validity of St. John's contention. There are equally powerful human arguments all around us. Many who are indifferent to God—if not outright hostile—are wonderful parents, spouses, and friends, loving at the highest human level without any awareness of or dependence on God. They have thriving marriages, happy and secure children, and deeply meaningful relationships. All of this, and no God making it happen.

We love because he first loved us? It is simply not true.

At least, not if our instrument of measure is merely human. If that is the extent of our sample then of course there will be limitless examples of people perfectly capable of love without even a glance in the direction of Christianity's mysterious tripartite deity. Perhaps, though, the truthfulness of John's statement cannot be accessed at the surface. Perhaps its currents run in deep waters out of eye's view. Genesis's creation account reports that when it came time to make the human race God determined to make humans in God's own image. There are numerous legitimate ways to understand what it means to be made in God's likeness, but certainly one aspect is that we reflect his nature.

And his nature, as we have said, is love. We were made in love, for love, by the One who is love. It is woven into our being to love; it is an inextricable component of what it means to be human. For all our capacity for cruel and selfish behaviors, it is in us to desire love and to give love to others. What explains this vital component of our createdness? What gives a man the ability to love a woman, a friend to lay down her life for her friend, a child to give his heart to his parents? What lies behind love's adamant expression and indefatigable efforts? Whether one is a devotee of Jesus, an avowed atheist, a Buddhist monk in a Tibetan monastery, or a radicalized Islamicist simultaneously loving his children while plotting the slaughter of the children of infidels, there is one answer: we love because he first loved us. The God who directs sunrises and sunsets is love; he loves all whom he has made; in love he made us in his likeness. Our capacity, drive, longing to love? It comes from him, from being made like him. Gandhi's ability to love his enemies? It came from the One who created Gandhi in his own image. Bill and Melinda Gates's heart for the diseased poor of the Third World?

That's their Father's heart, whether or not they know and acknowledge him as Father. Love is a resource traceable to only one wellspring: God.

When we love we love out of God's limitless resources. None of it can be traced back to us; there is no innate kindness or charity that we possess on our own that can account for love's presence in our lives. We do not love out of ourselves, out of the riches of our own character, the tenderness of our own hearts, or the calculation of our own determination to love. None of the love we give or express originates in us.

So the prophet renowned for his sensitivity of heart and the frequency of his tears says (Jeremiah 17:9 ESV), "The heart is deceitful above all things and desperately sick; who can understand it?" We like to flatter ourselves as being good and loving when kind impulses overtake us and find expression through us; in fact there is nothing good in us that can be credited to us. Not a single thing. Jesus sees this and speaks it plainly. When a man greets him with the honorific "Good Teacher," Jesus offers an immediate rejoinder. "Why do you call me good? No one is good except God alone" (Mark 10:17-18 ESV). Jesus' response to the man startles the attentive reader. Jesus refuses to describe himself as good, nor will he allow others to do so. He insists all goodness resides solely in God. So what possible grounds can we have for claiming personal achievement in goodness? *We* are good? Really? When even the sinless Son of the Father declines the identification, he who among all who ever adorned human flesh was good if anyone ever was?

Perhaps we need to rethink our position.

We love because he first loved us. Not: we love because we are fundamentally good. Not: we love because we willed to do so. Not: we love because our hearts are essentially noble and altruistic.

Love. What can explain it? Only this: God, who tirelessly and compassionately loves all whom he has made, puts his own nature as love inside of us. We love because he first loved us, whether we love him or not, whether we like it or not. Sinner or saint, kingdom advocate or committed pagan, each time love makes its mark in and through us, there is only one explanation: God. He made us in love, for love, and even in this upside down world of increasing depravity, love finds a way. When it does, its route can always be traced back to him.

Each time an agnostic moves in kindness toward another human being, that's God in her. Each time an atheist lays down his life for a lover, friend, or countryman, that's God in him. Each time an irreligious person takes time to be with someone the world has discarded or marginalized, that's God in him. Each time a witch or wiccan brings peace and speaks affirmation to a broken life, that's God in her. Each time a follower of Joseph Smith puts his family first and his own desires second, that's God in him. Each time a Unitarian-Universalist physician sacrifices to bring healing to the poor and forgotten, that's God in her.

Each time, every time love finds a way, there is only one way to account for it: we love because he first loved us.

Why Follow Jesus, Then?

If that's true, then what advantage is there to being a follower of Jesus? If all love always comes back to the Father regardless of whether we set him apart in our hearts as such, what does it matter if we welcome Christ as Lord?

There are advantages to knowing Christ on many fronts. Our eternal destiny, the meaning of our existence here on earth, the healing of deepest hurts—knowing Christ carries significant, unique upsides. But as it specifically relates to the release and increase of love, the advantage lies here. When we permit Christ to take up residence in our lives, when we give way to his Spirit's transformation of our hearts, then the One whose fullness fills all things in every way (Ephesians 1:23 HCSB) fills us. The more his life gets into us, the more his life gets out of us, and its foremost manifestation is love. The increase of the Lord in us is evidenced by an increase of his love escaping from our lives and flooding into the lives of others. This is why Jesus can say that the world will know we belong to him by our remarkable love. Not because we're better than anyone else but because he is better than anyone else, and he is in us. The psalmist sings, "Your love is better than life," and what we see when we look at Jesus is that his love is our life. It is everything.

Paul explains in Romans the dreadful consequences of failing to welcome the love of God into our lives. What happens, he says, is this. When we reject God and distance ourselves from him, when we refuse to give him his rightful place as God and set ourselves up as the lords of our own little fiefdoms, we move farther and farther away from our true nature as people created in love, for love. Instead of the straight way, we find ourselves increasingly on twisted roads that lead to the distortion of God's nature within us. Our thoughts begin to resemble the roads we've chosen, twisted and perilous, and our actions follow suit. The thing we're made for, love, is squeezed out by dishonorable passions and darkened pursuits. Now and again love finds a way even in these forsaken environs, but it is rarer and rarer. Pretty soon we cannot remember that we were made for a better, higher life; indeed, over time we forget that we have a Creator at all. As Paul describes it, the results are catastrophic. "Refusing to know God, we soon didn't know how to be human either—women didn't know how to be women, men didn't know how to be men. Sexually confused, we abused and defiled one another, women with women, men with men—all lust, no love. And then we paid for it, oh, how we paid for it—emptied of God and love, godless and loveless wretches."[50]

What advantage to following Jesus? Simply this: following him reconnects us with what it means to be human, authentically and truly alive as daughters and sons of a Father whose love claims us and brims over our lives. What advantage? Simply this: eternal life ensues from knowing and enjoying him. Jesus defines eternal life not as a place we go when we die but a Person to whom we come in order to really live. "This is eternal life," he announces,

---

[50] Romans 1:26-27 MSG (adapted).

"to know you, the only true God, and Jesus Christ whom you have sent" (John 17:3). Eternal life starts now, not later, and love is its defining characteristic.

This, then, is the ultimate test for the dangerous kind: love. As their affair is waning in Woody Allen's classic 1977 film, Alvy Singer tells his girlfriend, Annie Hall, "A relationship, I think, is like a shark, you know? It has to constantly move forward or it dies. And I think what we got on our hands is a dead shark."[51] The dangerous kind know this truth: if we are not known for our outrageous love then what we've got on our hands is a dead shark.

What's love got to do with it? Well, as it applies to Christianity, love is not just an ingredient in what will be served to our guests, it is the whole meal. When the world cannot identify love in us, especially when making honest efforts to find it, something is fatally wrong. Any attempt to point the way into generous, dangerous living with God is absurdly incomplete if it does not insist on love as the preeminent feature of following Christ.

Love Is Not Ethereal

Love is not ethereal. It is not an emotion. It is not a sentiment we express when we are moved to do so. Love is action. When Scripture describes God as loving the whole world, filthy and fallen though it is, love is not offered as a feeling in God's heart that motivates him to a kindly disposition toward us. The evidence of God's love is not that he feels good about us. The proof of heaven's love is this: he sent his beloved Son Jesus as the flawless revelation of his heart to die for our sins that we might find our way back into true friendship with him. Love is self-giving in the extreme. It holds nothing back and leaves no one out. It does not take its lead from how or whether it is received, acknowledged, or appreciated. It is

---

[51] *Annie Hall*, Woody Allen, director. Written by Woody Allen and Marshall Brickman. (United Artists, 1977).

indefatigable—it keeps coming and coming and coming. Nothing can stop or slow it. Not even death.

Its expression is concrete. The Bible leaves no room for love to be understood as an abstract concept or as a rhetorical device. "Dear friends, do you think you'll get anywhere in this if you learn all the right words but never do anything?" James, Jesus' brother asks (James 2:14-17 MSG). "For instance, you come upon an old friend dressed in rags and half-starved and say, 'Good morning, friend! Be clothed in Christ! Be filled with the Holy Spirit!' and walk off without providing so much as a coat or a cup of soup—where does that get you? Isn't it obvious that God-talk without God-acts is outrageous nonsense?" In the community of the redeemed, especially among the dangerous kind, the outrageous nonsense of God-talk without God-acts is not tolerated. It is exposed for what it is—a rank fraud—and dismissed. Love—the real thing, the true thing, the thing with skin on that finds a way every time—is esteemed and pursued as the highest life God has to offer. In fact, it is the only life God offers. Anything less is not his life at all.

This brings us back to the observation that, as a general rule, Christians are not widely admired for their outrageous love and selfless, nonjudgmental ways. If this is right it tells us something unsettling: the life we are living is less than the life God has for us. Those who are in Christ, who by virtue of having been wooed by his irresistible kindness and astonishing yearning for them, will be marked as his not by the bumper stickers on their cars or the scriptural slogans on their t-shirts, but by love: great love for God and real love for the world. The love that is in them is Christ himself and it must get out of them because this is what love does: it finds a way.

And if, as at times will be the case, we are rejected and the love of God in us is refused, we will not be bothered. We will not react. And not because we have risen imperiously above such common responses. No, if love has taught us anything, surely it has taught us this: we are not above anything or anyone. We will not react to rejection because nothing can touch the richness of what our Father has deposited in us. No threat will cause us to cower, no difficulty will entice us to throw in the towel, no ridicule will get us to agree to give up our premiere kingdom assignment—to love as if our hearts are on fire.

The Holy Spirit: How Love Finds a Way

How shall we do this, love as if our hearts are on fire? Intrinsically self-absorbed and selfish as we are, how will we become lovers in a perilous age? How will God's love ever find its way out of us?

First it must find its way into us. Love always finds a way, and this is its way: the Holy Spirit. Going to church, commendable though it may be, is not the way. Conducting thorough-going etymological studies of the Greek words for love, interesting as this might prove, won't get it done. Gaining the wisdom of psychiatrists, counselors, and psychotherapists, illuminating as this might be, is not the way. Sitting at the feet and learning from the experiences of those well-versed in love, edifying as this may turn out for us, will not get it done. No human approach can open the reservoir and release the floodgates of love. Only God can do that.

So Paul tells his friends in Rome, "God has poured out his love into our hearts by the Holy Spirit, whom he has given us" (Romans 5:5b NIV). Perhaps this lies behind Paul's insistence that when it comes to experiencing the presence and life of the Holy Spirit, once is not enough. Because Holy Spirit Highway is the only avenue God's love accesses to make its travels through our lives, Paul exhorts Jesus' friends to "Make the most of every chance you get. These are desperate times! Don't live carelessly, unthinkingly. Make sure you understand what the Master wants. Don't drink too much wine. That cheapens your life. Drink the Spirit of God, huge draughts of him" (Ephesians 5:16-18 MSG). *Drink the Spirit of God, huge draughts of him!* In other words, drink until you cannot take another sip, until you overflow with him, until you are saturated and waterlogged with him. Do so—and this is especially important—continually, over and over again, hour by hour, day after day. Paul's command to be filled is in the present imperative tense, indicating an ongoing, constant experience of filling. "We were all given the one Spirit to drink," Paul tells the Corinthian believers (1 Corinthians 12:13 NIV), and his advice to every follower of Jesus is to drink up and keep drinking because that's where the life is. And where the life is, love is.

This is why the Holy Spirit is so important in the life of the dangerous kind. Not because miracles, healings, tongues, and rapturous spiritual experiences follow in his wake—though when the Father gives these gifts, we receive them with glad hearts as an expression of his goodness and holiness—but because where the Holy Spirit invades, the life and love of Jesus are established. This is what the Holy Spirit does, the only thing he does: he brings Jesus front and center.

Jesus, describing the fundamental nature and function of the Holy Spirit, said, "When the Spirit of truth comes, he will guide you into all truth. He will not speak on his own but will tell you what he has heard. He will tell you about the future. He will bring me glory by telling you whatever he receives from me" (John 16:13-14 NLT). The Spirit never draws attention to himself, his own activity, his own teaching. He is consumed with Jesus and with seeing praise, honor, and glory come to him. This is the character of the Holy Spirit, as J. I. Packer notes: "He functions as a floodlight trained on Christ, so that it is Christ, not the Spirit, whom we see." He works in us with this goal in view, that we who were created to be to the praise of Jesus' glory would become more and more like the Father's Son.[52]

Consequently, we test the veracity of our claim to be Spirit-filled and the accuracy of our teaching and thinking about the Holy Spirit the same way. Do we bring glory to Jesus Christ? Do our theological formulations and our statements about the Holy Spirit

---

[52] J. I. Packer, *Affirming the Apostles' Creed* (Wheaton, IL: Crossway Books, 2008), Kindle location 975-83; compare Ephesians 1:12.

bring Jesus into focus? Is our implacable resolve to see glory and honor come to the Son who is the Father's delight? If so, then it can be said of us that we have rivers of living water running through us. Because we have taken long, thirsty drinks of the Holy Spirit, and because we keep returning to the fountain for more, we increasingly resemble the Firstborn of all creation. And, consequently, the gold standard of the Christian life, love, manifests and expresses itself through us. Not because we are good but because he is, and he lives in us.

It stands to reason: the more like Jesus we are, the more Jesus' love will pour into us and from us. The more the Holy Spirit has his way with us, the more love will find a way through us to a world that is looking for Christians who remind them of Jesus. "And the Lord—who is the Spirit—," writes Paul, "makes us more and more like him as we are changed into his glorious image" (2 Corinthians 3:18 NLT). Modern disciples who remind outside observers of Jesus? That's normal for the dangerous kind. Being people who love like our hearts are on fire? That's normal, too, for the dangerous kind. Not because we have arduously trained ourselves, conquered our hearts, and finally figured out the mystery of love. No. Loving like Jesus loves has nothing to do with us and our aptitude for kindness, compassion, and charity. Rather, it can be traced to a baffling, wondrous, marvelous truth: love came down and made its home inside of us. This and nothing else is the essence of the Christian life.

What's love got to do with it?

The dangerous kind know the answer to this question.

Everything.

Repent — Kingdom Life Starts Here

Repentance is an essential and unexpected factor in maximum kingdom living and in becoming the dangerous kind. If this is not an easy sell or an immediately attractive option for us, it is not surprising. Because repentance, ruthless and thoroughgoing repentance, can only adorn a life that is truly under the word of Christ. As we have seen, we do not like to be under anything. We prefer to be on top of everything. Repentance is the ultimate under, placing us as it does under the Holy Spirit's convicting work, under his insistent redirecting of our lives, our energies, our outcomes.

Repentance is unqualified confession that we are wrong. We'd rather be right, and when we are not, we'd prefer no one else know about it. If they know it and see it and have it irrefutably confirmed, then they will also identify this in us: weakness. Not a winsome, charming, Chicago-Cubs-as-lovable-losers weakness, but a shattering revelation of moral and spiritual failure. Repentance is the peeling away of the layers of our self-satisfaction and self-sufficiency. It reveals that all our pretty adornments are but ragged Salvation Army castoffs. It shows, ultimately, that we are naked. For all our preening, parading, and posing, repentance exposes us. It shows us true. It shows us to be naked. And if there is one way we do not want to go public, it's like that. Naked.

But the dangerous kind are dangerous because they are willing to be exposed. They pursue it. They insist on it. The dangerous kind know, when it comes down to it, that their fundamental condition is one of weakness and need. They do not operate from a position of personal strength or piety. They move, live, and have their being within this reality: apart from humble submission to and radical dependence on the tender mercies of Christ, they are wretched and miserable and poor and blind and naked (Revelation 3:17 NLT).

This picture is not flattering. Our culture does not value it. We like our heroes mighty and magnificent, invulnerable and invincible. We thrill to shows of strength, to exhibitions of valor in which the antagonist is dispatched with extreme prejudice. We love the man who walks into a bar full of outlaw bikers, a human harbinger of justice, who is going to clear the room, break some bones, spill some blood. In our movies and in our daydreams, our champion may or may not be all that much to look at, but he is gallant and grounded and good, and always, always, always when the dust settles he is the last man standing. We'll take the Terminator over Teresa and the Calcutta lepers every day of the week.

The thing of it is, though, when it comes to spiritual virility and kingdom impact, the last man standing is the loser. Because while Scripture is replete with encouragements to stand in the faith, stand in the face of adversity, and stand when collapsing and quitting are the easier way to go, standing is not the starting point of the Christian life. Kneeling is. Falling prostrate before the Lord of heaven and earth is. The dangerous kind are acutely aware that unless they begin *here* they will never stand *there*. The last man standing is the man who refuses to kneel, who will not acknowledge the absolute claim of Christ on his life, who thinks he can sin and get away with it without injuring his character and call and credibility, who thinks repentance is a great idea for everyone else. That's why the last man standing is the last man you want standing next to you when the gloves are off and the pressure's on. Because the fire that reveals all things for what they really are—the fire of trouble and trial and tribulation and testing—that fire will burn him up and burn his house down. Eventually we learn this: no matter how profound his earthly success, how powerful his gifting, or potent his preaching, the last man standing turns out to be a mirage, mere wood, hay, and stubble that gets consumed in a moment.

The first man kneeling, that's who we want to be next to. Actually, it is who we want to be, who we must be ourselves if we are to be dangerous for the King and his kingdom.

Isaiah: A Thoroughly Dangerous Man

Isaiah may be seen as a leading edge and exemplar of what dangerous following after God looks like. He is a thoroughly dangerous man. Coined "the Shakespeare of the prophets" by scholars for his eloquence and literary accomplishment, he is especially notable for his detailed messianic prophecies. The future for all humankind comes rushing into view as Isaiah reveals the heart of God and heaven's strategy for calling a wandering world back to the One whose tenderness ever pursues her. Isaiah's voice is clear and unequivocal; he spares no one's feelings, he safeguards no fragile spiritual sensibilities. With no apology or qualification he makes sweeping condemnations of sin and announcements of God's redeeming justice. Though at times a friend of royal courts, he is not universally revered. But even the most ferocious opposition cannot silence him, nor can the most terrifying threats shut him down. Isaiah is bold, brilliant, and courageous to the last, though his end is bitter indeed. Talmudic tradition tells us that his enemies sawed him in half during Manasseh's reign of unprecedented violence and bloodshed.

What makes him so dangerous is not that he was the last man standing but that he was the first man kneeling. Isaiah was commissioned for his life's work in the midst of his most famous vision, the throne of the living God and the angelic throngs of heaven. His description of it and of the angels' song is evocative: "They were calling out to each other, 'Holy, holy, holy is the Lord of Heaven's

Armies! The whole earth is filled with his glory!' Their voices shook the Temple to its foundations, and the entire building was filled with smoke" (Isaiah 6:3-4 NLT).

Isaiah's next move is instructive. He does not immediately organize a conference where he and his fellow prophetic supervoices can describe their experiences and coach the masses into having their own visions, revelations, and open heaven visitations. He does not establish a Glory Vision School in which he tutors spiritually hungry students in how to cultivate their own throne room experiences. He does not author a spiritual self-help book entitled *Accessing the Throne Zone* in which he seeks to elevate people's pedestrian experiences of God into encounters so overwhelming and incomprehensible that words are inadequate to convey. He does none of these things.

Isaiah's next move is his only move and it is the move against which all claims to having been taken up into the heavenly realms must be measured: he repents. The holiness of God is so saturating that Isaiah's sin has nowhere to hide. Not unlike the demons who would cry out when Jesus showed up, Isaiah's sin—secret and submerged and safe in the darkness—rises up and is outed. Consequently, these words pour forth before Isaiah has a chance to clamp his hands over his mouth.

> Woe is me, for I am ruined!
> Because I am a man of unclean lips,
> And I live among a people of unclean lips;
> For my eyes have seen the King, the Lord of hosts
> (Isaiah 6:5 NASB).

"Doom! It's Doomsday! I'm as good as dead!" is Eugene Peterson's paraphrase of the prophet's dismay. God's warning to Moses some 700 years earlier was stark and not open to misinterpretation, and Isaiah would have known it well. "No one may see me and live" (Exodus 33:20b NLT). Angelic visitations in Scripture are often accompanied by the immediate reassurance, "Do not be afraid!" and on occasion their appearance results in fainting for those receiving them.[53] A true God-visitation, on the other hand, results in the fainter being knocked out cold forever; one might say a dead faint ensues. Being slain in the Spirit takes on new meaning when God himself shows up on the scene or when he draws a person up into the scene in heaven.

Thus Isaiah's first and only possible response, and the thing that will make him so dangerous subsequently. He's the first man kneeling. He repents. It is this willingness to sit first, simply to be in the presence of the Lord, which will enable Isaiah to walk out his kingdom assignment later on and ultimately to stand when his adversaries come to take his life. Isaiah's testimony is echoed in Paul's theology. Isaiah enters the realm of glory and his involuntary response is, "I'm a dead man!" So Paul says, "For he raised us from the dead along with Christ, and now we are seated with him in the heavenly realms" (Ephesians 2:6 NIV). This is what transpires for Isaiah. He's lost, ruined, a dead man, for he has seen the Lord and his sinfulness has been exposed. In a sense Isaiah truly does die right there, and it is the mercy and grace of God that bring him back to life: "Then one of the seraphim flew to me with a burning coal he had taken from the altar with a pair of tongs. He touched my lips with it and said, 'See, this coal has touched your lips. Now your guilt is removed, and your sins are forgiven'" (Isaiah 6:6-7 NLT). Repentance proves to be the antidote for the lethal venom of Isaiah's sin. His first move is the best move; it sets him up for the future God has appointed for him.

Our own ideas about repentance tend to be, well, wrong. We think of it as the guilty feelings we get when we no longer can get away with indulging ourselves in an inferior life and the accompanying confession of the wrong we have done. We fear repentance because it is the result of an exposure we'd rather not suffer, an outing of the things that contradict the life of Christ in us. Too often when we repent (or merely hear the call to do it) what we really hear is that we have done the BAD THING, and shame on us for that! It's not surprising that we run and hide, filled with shame and dread

---

[53] As it did for Daniel (10:4ff).

that we will be discovered as someone engaging in the BAD THING. Fear mounts a rapacious attack and our inner demons launch a malicious campaign. Soon we are not just someone who has done the BAD THING, we *are* the BAD THING. So we run. We hide. We cover up. We deny. Repentance? It must be avoided at all costs if we are to escape the torture we fear awaits us at the hands of the moral and spiritual KGB.

No One Repents in Hell

In that state, are we likely to repent? *There's no way in hell we're going to repent.* This is literally true. When we fear exposure, believing it will mean rejection and personal repudiation, we are in hell. When we are stuck in life-stealing behaviors or are losing strength in the face of temptation and we fear breathing a word of it to anyone for the judgments we will endure, we are in hell. When we've persuaded ourselves that we don't just *do* bad things but that we *are* the BAD THING, we are in hell. And in hell no one repents. It's simply not encouraged. It never occurs to us that it is an option, and this is by design. The enemy's design. No one repents in hell because that's the nature of the beast; despair, depression, and deception are the beast's nature, and he uses them to keep us in his lair. So by the time we're in hell we assume it's a little late in the game to repent.

In hell no one's dangerous, no one's a threat to the purposes of the adversary, no one's potent for the Lord of the angel armies. In hell we are disarmed, disabled, and disqualified. Hell is right where the enemy of our soul wants us. He's the one who led us there, his lies and fear mongering festering like cankerous soul-sores. We fear repentance because Old Scratch has put it into our hearts to fear it. He knows the truth, though of course he'll never let us in on it, that if we repent we won't die. We'll live. We'll be restored, released, remade, renewed. This, too, is the truth, and Beelzebub is of no mind to disclose it: in our sin we're already dead. We're not *going* to die; we're already dead. Certainly this is Paul's view of things (Ephesians 2:1, 4-5 HCSB). "And you were dead in your trespasses and sins…but God, who is rich in mercy, because of His great love that He had for us, made us alive with the Messiah even though we were dead in trespasses. You are saved by grace!"

The deadly power of sin is manifold. When we sin we fear being found out. Like the first man and the first woman, we believe it just may be possible to hide. We think it just may be possible to outrun our sin and its exposure of us, so run we do. We believe we are preserving ourselves as we attempt our escape, never realizing that we have become animated corpses making laps around the graveyard. We cannot see that we will not live unless Someone breathes life into us again. To our eternal fortune, that Someone pursues us single-mindedly, all the way to the cemetery and back, determined that sin and death will not have the final say over us. That Someone recognizes the devices of the Devourer; he hates them and he hates him with an everlasting hatred, and he will not rest until his love has won us over and set us free and resurrected us forever.

And so the first man kneeling wins. The one who repents kneels before the King of Righteousness and lives. The sinner who repents is not shamed by the Father he runs to for being the BAD THING. The sinner who repents discovers the One he runs to is outrunning him to meet in a life-giving, destiny preserving embrace. Those who repent are no longer in hell, no longer on the lam from the long arm of the Law. Repentance is release and it is God's word of hope set against all the destroying words of our enemy. When Satan's sly, savage whispers assault our hearts with accusations of being disqualified and a disappointment to God, the Word over all words declares these dark words null and void.

This is why the writer of Hebrews argues so ardently for a life of eschewing sin and for coming boldly into the throne room of God for mercy when we do sin. "Let us strip off every weight that slows us down, especially the sin that so easily trips us up. And let us run with endurance the race God has set before us. We do this by keeping our eyes on Jesus, the champion who initiates and perfects our faith....Further, since we have a great High Priest set over the household of God, let us draw near with true hearts and fullest confidence, knowing that our inmost souls have been purified by the sprinkling of his blood" (Hebrews 12:1b-2a NLT; 10:21-22 PHILLIPS). John, Jesus' closest friend and confidante, adds his hearty agreement. "My dear children, I am writing this to you so that you will not sin. But if anyone does sin, we have an advocate who pleads our case before the Father. He is Jesus Christ, the one who is truly righteous. He himself is the sacrifice that atones for our sins—and not only our sins but the sins of all the world" (1 John 2:1-2 NLT).

Repentance Makes Us Dangerous

Isaiah is dangerous. His starting point, repentance, makes him so. Previous to this vision he lived with the same self-satisfaction as the general population. Sure, he wasn't perfect but no one is, and at the end of the day he was a good man doing a good work for the good Lord. He has an appropriate sense of humanity's fallenness (see 1:15-17), God's beauty and holiness (see 4:2-6, and the unassailable justice of the Lord (see 5:9-16). But in his unparalleled revelation of the Lord on his throne all these things become immediate and personal for Isaiah. It's his own fallenness he sees, not humanity's. He gazes on the Lord whose glory outfires a thousand suns, and he sees that glory in bleak contrast to his own sin. He moves from a theology of God's judgment on the sin of nations to the raw terror of perceiving that he is subject to that same justice and righteous judgment.

When Isaiah cries out at his impending doom, the weight of his sinfulness crushing him like a millstone, he falls to the ground because he can do no other thing. He's not the last man standing. He's the first man kneeling. And if this occasioned by an instinct for self-preservation, by having gone involuntarily weak in the knees, no matter. This is what matters: for the first time, he sees himself clearly. He's a dead man. He only *thought* he was living before. He entered heaven dead in his trespasses. He emerges fully alive for the purposes of the One who knew him in his mother's womb. When he goes in, his sins are like scarlet and as red as crimson; when he comes out they are as white as snow, like the finest wool.[54] Years later, when his prophetic career is mature and in full bloom, he will say, "We all, like sheep, have gone astray, each of us has turned to his own way" (Isaiah 53:6a NIV). It is an observation hard won as the result of his experience of God's glory. When he says "all," he includes himself; his statement is offered not as propositional truth but as personal confession.

Because he is a man who once was blind but now can see, he is a threat to Satan's cruel designs. Truly alive because the Father has touched and forgiven him, the powers of hell cannot prevail against him. No accusation of the enemy will find purchase, no attempt to crush him with condemnation will succeed. Until in tenderness and affection his Father says, "You can stop now, my son. Isaiah, it's time to come home," Isaiah is unstoppable.

This is the work product of repentance, of being the first man kneeling instead of the last man standing. The net yield of repentance is freedom, release, power, life, and the exponential increase of our danger quotient. Satan's efforts to seat us at his sinful buffet where we will develop an appetite for hellish perversions and distortions has less to do with specific sinful activities than with a determination to render us spiritually impotent. At all costs we must not be allowed to become dangerous. Sin is crippling to strategic discipleship because it converts us into people who run away from God rather than to him. It makes us hiders instead of abiders.

We are so stupid! We laser in on the particularities of sin, the activities we're so shamefully engaged in, as if in and of themselves they are Satan's real objective. They are not. They are merely devices of darkness; they are not the darkness itself. The darkness is separation from light and life. What our adversary is after is not getting us to sin, though this is a wicked delight for him, but in separating us from the One we were always made to love. Separated from the

---

[54] Compare Isaiah 1:18b.

Lover of our soul we cannot engage the kingdom life he intends us to live, nor occupy the territory he has appointed for us to possess.

The Rest of Our Story

When Paul sets out the rhythm of the Christian life in Ephesians, he begins with rest. Once dead in our sins, we have been raised with Christ and are now seated with him in the heavenly realms (Ephesians 2:6). The importance of being seated with Christ should not be missed by the dangerous kind. Seated we are at rest. We are not striving, struggling, succumbing, or succeeding. We are *with* him. That is all, and that is enough. There, seated, Jesus is the entirety of our orientation. When we are with him, he is all we want; he is our total fascination and we discover that we are his delight. There, seated with him and at rest, he can have his way with us. There, uninterrupted and undivided, his fellowship with us begins to stir in us all that he has placed within us that will make us dangerous when we set our feet to walk in his way. There, in that place of rest, he shakes us, wrecks us, makes us, moves us, kisses us, holds us, loves us, disciplines us, leads us, shows us, proves us, captivates us, refreshes us, challenges us, corrects us, reassures us, equips us, builds us, finds us, sends us. The one who kneels first wins because repentance is the entryway to God's rest, where the best of who he is and what he has for us can be tasted and experienced. This is Isaiah's discovery, a great secret shared with him by the One who surprised him with merciful atonement in his heavenly vision. "This is what the Sovereign Lord, the Holy One of Israel, says: 'In repentance and rest is your salvation, in quietness and trust is your strength'" (Isaiah 30:15 NIV).

Watchman Nee, leader of an indigenous underground church movement in China and considered so dangerous by Chinese authorities that he was imprisoned for the last twenty years of his life until his death in 1972, draws attention to the same unusual spiritual reality that Isaiah discovered. "Our natural reason says, 'What can we attain without effort? How can we get anywhere if we do not move?' But Christianity is a queer business! If at the outset we try to do anything, we get nothing; if we seek to attain something, we miss everything."[55] Most unexpectedly, our life with God begins not with acting and accomplishing but with rest. We see this in the order of creation. God fashions the heavens and the earth in just under a week; he works for six days and rests on the seventh. This last day of the creation story is the first full day of Adam's story. Shaped from dust on day six, he enjoys all that has come from the hand of his Maker for the first time on day seven, resting with the One who himself is at rest. Our beginning, spiritually speaking, is in rest. In repentance and rest is our salvation and strength, and here we will find the resources for the next part of our journey with Christ, walking.

Our rest, which is the beginning point for the kingdom life we've been invited into, springs from repentance. Significantly, when Jesus issues the summons to walk with him and be immersed in the kingdom life that is breaking in all around him, his invitation is conveyed with a one word command: repent (Matthew 4:17 NIV). *"Repent, for the kingdom of heaven is near!"* So many things he could have said, so many words he might have used to introduce his earthly ministry, and the one he chooses is repent.

Had he been surrounded by media consultants, his handlers would have stroked out. "No, no, Jesus! Not *repent*, not that word as your first word," they'd surely have advised him. "*Repent*—that's the sort of thing you have to work up to gently, slowly. You have to start with the soft sell, Jesus; that's the way to draw a crowd, and that's how you'll reel them in. First, tell them about heaven and angels and streets paved with gold. People *love* that stuff! Then tell them all the good things you're going to do for them here on earth; remember, Son, that when it comes to following you, people are always going to demand to know what's in it for them, and it better be good. So sell it, Jesus. Woo them with clever stories, especially ones that make their leaders look like buffoons. Trust us on this one—the masses

---

[55] Watchman Nee, *Sit, Walk, Stand* (Wheaton, IL: Tyndale, 1977), 14.

will eat it up! Next, grab their attention with thrilling miracles—open some blind eyes, raise a few people from the dead...you've got a gift for that sort of thing, and people love special effects. Then, when you have 'em right where you want 'em, eating out of the palm of your hand, that's when you spring the trap. That's when you speak the word repent. Not as your first word but—if you absolutely insist on throwing it in, which we'd advise against—as your last."

Maybe we'd do it that way but Jesus does not. He cannot. He does not save this word for last. It must be spoken first, before all other words. Every other word he speaks will be set against the backdrop of this one word. In fact, what he says later will make little sense and will not achieve its intended purpose if this word is not spoken and attended to first.

Repent. Kingdom life starts here. Importantly, Jesus' first word is not a new word. His cousin, John the Baptizer, proclaimed the same message in his forerunner ministry. John and Jesus stand in continuity with a long prophetic tradition in which the best life God has for us cannot be accessed any other way than this: "Repent and live!" This is the fulcrum of Peter's Pentecost sermon as well, in response to which 3,000 people leave their old ways and attach themselves to the One who is the Way. "Repent and be baptized, every one of you," Peter urges the throng that has gathered in curiosity following the chaotic invasion of heaven among the friends of Jesus. What is going on, they wonder, and how can we get in on it?

Repent. This first and central word, heard and heeded, will cause us to be the first ones kneeling in humility rather than the last ones standing in stubborn commitment to self-reliance. Repentance is self-reliance's utter opposite. To repent is to opt for self-preservation and its result is a lush life with God. In repentance and rest is our salvation; in quietness and trust is our strength. The promise of Scripture is that repentance will replenish what Satan and the flesh have depleted. "Repent, then, and turn to God," Peter advises those who've come running to ogle the crippled beggar who is healed at the temple gate, "so that your sins may be wiped out, that times of refreshing may come from the Lord" (Acts 3:18 NIV).

On the whole, our understanding and experience of repentance—when we're cornered and cannot escape it—is confined almost exclusively to the first aspect of Peter's encouragement. Our repenting is rarely done with a view toward the second. As reluctant as we are to admit our sinfulness, we need our sins wiped out and we know it. The Bible tells us so, and so did every Sunday School teacher we ever had. We need our guilt lifted off and our shame repealed. Hand-fashioned in the image of the Ancient of Days, sin is not an adornment we were designed to wear. It never looks good on us. But our capacity to see this has been diminished as we walk in a world of fading light. Not only we but everyone around us is wearing the same tattered rags, and we imagine them to be handsome. Until our Helper breaks through and breaks us out of our dark bondage we do not realize that the daughters and sons of the King were never meant to wear pauper's garments. When we repent we are remade, our inner compass is recalibrated, and we get a fresh start without the burden of our sin dragging us under the foul tide of brackish waters. Instead, rivers of living water spring up within us; the sin that was damming the flow has been flushed out and washed away. Once garbed in sin's impoverished rags, now we are robed in Christ's own brilliant righteousness. Our sad, unlovely nakedness is covered over; Jesus now clothes us with himself (Ephesians 4:22-24; Galatians 3:27).

Repentance is about sin. Our sin. We get that. What we may miss, however, is that repentance is also about refreshment. Genesis reports that before sin sabotaged Adam and Eve in the garden, they walked with God in the cool of the day. Every day was for them a time of refreshing as they walked companionably with the One who made them and delighted in them. But Satan infiltrated paradise and corrupted Eden's children. Lucifer's seed germinated, blossomed, and sprang forth in a rank harvest of darkness, disobedience, and death. And just that fast the times of refreshing were over. Never again would creation's first man and first woman walk unselfconsciously in their nakedness with the Lord. That recreation had been stolen and destroyed by the one whose special talents lay in thievery and destruction. Sin's treachery is not just that it introduces death where life once held sway but that it robs us of this primeval joy: unrestricted, unlimited times of refreshing in the presence of the Lord.

This, too, is why we rush to join our lives to the surprising first word of Jesus' announcement of the kingdom. "Repent!" he cries, not because he is a cosmic killjoy but because he knows sin is a joy killer. "Repent!" he trumpets, not because he is obsessed with sin but because he is obsessed with life. "Repent!" he calls, because he knows that on this narrow way is our rest and strength recovered. The Son of Man who came to obliterate all the works of the devil comes also to restore what was lost in the garden, times of refreshing with the Lord. Because of Jesus' kindness and great love, when the sons of Adam and daughters of Eve rally to his call to repent, they are released to walk again in the cool of the day with their friend and Father.

"Repent and live!" Ezekiel decrees.

"Repent, for the kingdom of heaven is near," John the Baptizer announces.

"The kingdom of God is near. Repent and believe the good news!" Jesus declares.

"Repent, then, and turn to God," Peter insists.

"God commands all people everywhere to repent," Paul preaches.

"Be earnest, and repent," demands the Living One who is the First and the Last.[56]

Why? Because kingdom life and dangerous living start here, with the first ones kneeling. They will be the last ones standing as well. Standing in faith and in fidelity to the King, these disciples will be potent for the purposes of God and a threat to the enemy of their soul because they have learned firsthand that repent is not just Jesus' first word, it is his best word.

---

[56] Ezekiel 18:32; Matthew 3:2; Mark 1:15; Acts 3:19; 17:30; Revelation 3:19.

Reckless

The dangerous kind are reckless.

Most of us, for most of our lives, have only ever understood this word pejoratively, associating it with great folly and great falls.

Adolph Hitler gambled everything with his invasion of Russia in June 1941. Code named Operation Barbarossa, the German attack was so successful initially that Hitler, greedy for the spoils of the resource rich Ukraine and made overconfident by his army's rapid advances, directed his forces away from Moscow. Instead of capturing Russia's capital city first and inflicting deep wounds in the Russian psyche, he went after the agricultural and oilfields of southern Russia. The result was a delay of over a month in the campaign against Moscow, with the German army stalling a mere seventeen miles outside of the great city. The winter of 1941-1942 was typically brutal. Temperatures plummeted to -81° Fahrenheit. The army, which had set out undersupplied for extreme temperatures, was exhausted and ill-equipped. "Men urinated on their freezing hands to warm them. The cracked skin bled with every movement. Soup that came boiling from the pot was frozen before it could be eaten. The tank engines could not be started. The recoil mechanisms of the guns froze, and fingers froze to exposed metal. The wounded or the exhausted who fell froze to death if they could not be roused into action."[57] The German army was done for. Instead of ordering his forces to dig in for winter, Hitler demanded they advance though he had not prepared for even the *chance* of winter warfare.

Reckless.

In 1995-1996, President Bill Clinton had consensual sexual contact with a twenty-two-year-old intern, Monica Lewinsky, on at least nine separate occasions. Though he denied her accusations of sexual misconduct, his sworn testimony was deemed false when Ms. Lewinsky produced a blue dress stained with the President's semen. Robert Reich, Clinton's labor secretary in his first term, said at the time that he couldn't fathom how Clinton could have taken such a risk. "In retrospect, the pattern [of the President's sexual dalliances] becomes clear. It makes the recklessness less understandable. Given the danger this has posed to his presidency, you'd think he'd take extra precautions against this compulsion." But President Clinton did not, and consequently, "we have a seriously crippled president for the next two years. He'll have a few good moments, he'll go through the motions, there will be adoring crowds, he'll use his bully pulpit and maybe he will have something he can call a victory. But essentially it's over."[58] Clinton was subsequently impeached by the House of Representatives, only the second impeachment of a president in American history. He was acquitted by the U.S. Senate in 1999 but the scandal nearly brought down a sitting American president and dominated headlines worldwide for two years. All for a few illicit sexual thrills.

Reckless.

Our associations with the word are rarely positive, in life and in Scripture.

---

[57] Bruce C. Paton, "Cold, Casualties, and Conquests: The Effects of Cold on Warfare," in *Medical Aspects of Harsh Environments, Volume 1* (U.S. Army Medical Department, The Borden Institute [http://www.bordeninstitute.army.mil/published_volumes/harshEnv1/harshenv1.html]), 329.

[58] Sally Quinn, "In Washington, That Letdown Feeling," *The Washington Post,* November 2, 1998 (http://www.washingtonpost.com [accessed June 18, 2011]).

When the angel of the Lord confronts Balaam, he explains his mission this way: "I have come here to oppose you because your path is a reckless one before me" (Numbers 22:32 NIV). When the residents of Shechem throw their support to Abimelech in his bid for Israel's throne, they give him money to raise a mercenary army. Scripture describes the men he hires as "worthless and reckless fellows" (Judges 9:4 NRSV).

Proverbs tells us that "a wise man fears the Lord and shuns evil but a fool is hotheaded and reckless," while Paul warns that in the last days recklessness will be a character flaw imbedded in a willful, godless generation (Proverbs 16:14 NIV; 2 Timothy 3:4 NLT).

It seems there is little to commend recklessness, which we understand as a wild carelessness paired with a foolish indifference to the consequences. When I was sixteen my buddy and I decided to see just how fast his father's new Camaro Z28 would go. We knew it was fast, of course. But how fast? There was only one way to find out. (Technically there were two: accepting the professional test results of the experts from *Road & Track* and *Car and Driver* or conducting our own road test, late at night on a lonely ribbon of highway outside town.) And we found out. His dad's muscle car topped out at an exhilarating 138 miles per hour.

Reckless. And dangerous.

When we say dangerous and reckless rarely do we use these two words in combination as a compliment. Dangerous, reckless people put themselves and others in harm's way, usually with a selfish, mindless disregard for the wellbeing of those around them. Foolhardy and self-absorbed, reckless people do not simply throw caution to the wind; they toss out common sense right along with it. Because they lack wisdom, discernment, perspective, and self-control they consistently cause trouble and find themselves knee deep in it. And they almost never seem to care. Putting others at risk, courting catastrophe at every turn, failing to value anyone's desires other than their own, their conduct does not register with themselves as either inappropriate or alarming. So they go along their way without the slightest concern for anyone in their way.

Reckless. It's a stupid, selfish, sinful way to live.

Usually.

There are some exceptions to the rule. There are instances when recklessness—a wild, calculated risk-taking indifferent to public opinion—is precisely what is called for. In the kingdom adventure Jesus invites his friends to embrace, reckless obedience to all that he commands makes them conspicuously dangerous to their adversary.

We see this play out again and again in Scripture. Abraham receives a bewildering instruction from the Lord: kill his only son, the son of the promise that all generations would be blessed through him. Already Abraham has exercised an insane faith, believing the word of God when, as a one-hundred-year-old man with a ninety-year-old wife, he trusted God to give him and Sarah a son. It was senseless to think it could happen, but "when everything was hopeless, Abraham believed anyway, deciding to live not on the basis of what he saw he *couldn't* do but on what God said he *would* do."[59] Then, when against every conceivable outcome he and Sarah actually did have a son, God shows up with a requirement that is at once heartbreaking and confounding. Abraham must offer his little boy as a human sacrifice to a God who will later go on record as regarding such practices as "detestable" and an "abomination" and a "profaning of his name" (Leviticus 18:21, 24-30; 2 Kings 23:20-25). This same God who insists Abraham make a human sacrifice of his son will later expressly forbid the practice: "There shall not be found among you anyone who burns his son or his daughter as an offering" (Deuteronomy 18:10a ESV). It is an impossible command to obey for any parent, no matter how much they love God, even if they are convinced, as Abraham was, "that if Isaac died God would bring him back to life again" (Hebrews 11:19a TLB). There's really only one word to describe Abraham's obedience on the mountain, arms outstretched, preparing to plunge the knife blade into his child's body.

Reckless.

---

[59] Romans 4:18a MSG (emphasis in original).

To those standing outside the community of God's covenant love, Abraham's obedience is worse than reckless. It is unconscionable. It is criminal. "Even though he didn't kill his son, it is still an incredibly cruel and evil thing to do," writes Chris Thiefe on his evilbible.com website. "If Abraham did that today he would be in jail serving a long sentence. It amazes me how Christians see this story as a sign of God's love. There is no love here, just pure, unadulterated evil."[60] Thiefe's passionate crucifixion of Abraham's behavior and of Christian belief will likely strike a chord among many atheists, agnostics, and postmodern rationalists. It's entirely reasonable that they would view the progenitor of Israel as a degenerate, deranged, delusional scoundrel.

This is the way of it for the dangerous kind. Reckless obedience is mystifying to the world. Our response to the voice of God will be at best enigmatic and at worst delusional when viewed through the eyes of those who stand outside the Christian faith. It won't make sense to them. It *can't* make sense to them, if Paul has rightly analyzed it. "For his Spirit searches out everything and shows us God's deep secrets," the apostle explains. "No one can know God's thoughts except God's own Spirit. And we have received God's Spirit (not the world's spirit), so we can know the wonderful things God has freely given us" (1 Corinthians 2:10b, 11b-12 NLT). The natural mind cannot apprehend supernatural realities; it can only assign them to categories of fantasy, magical thinking, and superstition. Without becoming people indwelled by the Holy Spirit, God's activity and our partnership with him will exceed what appears reasonable or rational. For those who spend most of their time in the context of Christian community it is easy to forget what we look like to those who are watching us from the outside. To them there is little difference between us and the gullible suckers who waste their paychecks on psychics and modern day shamans. See it for a moment from their vantage point – other than the de-

---

[60] Chris Thiefe, "Ritual Human Sacrifice in the Bible," www.evilbible.com/Ritual_Human_Sacrifice. htm (accessed July 6, 2011).

gree of recklessness, what is the difference between us and the poor deluded souls who drank Jim Jones's Kool-Aid?

For a certain segment of the population this is the way sold-out followers of Jesus appear. There's nothing new in this, of course. Biblical narratives offer a virtual buffet of men and women whose reckless obedience must have perplexed onlookers.

- Gideon emerges from obscurity—as the least man in the weakest clan of his tribe—to become a great military hero whose God-directed plan for defeating the numberless hordes of Midian was laughable: a force reduction of his troops from 32,000 to 300, armed not with swords and clubs but with torches, trumpets, and clay jars (Judges 7).
- Joshua receives marching orders from God that hardly qualify as classic military strategy: take the mighty, walled city of Jericho by marching around it once a day for six days, seven times on the seventh day with the ark of the covenant in the war train, and then instruct the priests to blow their ram's horns and the people to shout as loud as they can. Then the walls will come crashing down and Jericho will be utterly ransacked (Joshua 6).
- A shepherd boy on an errand for his father hears a giant taunting the armies of Israel and defaming her God. He offers to fight and slay the Philistine, confidently assuring Israel's terrified king, "I've killed both lions and bears and I'll do the same to this pagan giant who has defied the armies of the living God." He goes out to meet his foe without armor and with only a slingshot and five smooth stones as a weapon—all because he is positive that the Lord he's been singing to while watching his flocks will give him victory (1 Samuel 17).
- An angel appears to a teenager and announces that God has chosen her to become pregnant by his Holy Spirit and give birth to the Messiah. Though she's a virgin engaged to be married, with no credible way to explain things to her

parents, her fiancé, or her friends, she believes the Lord and consents to be his handmaiden (Luke 1:26–38).

• Jesus believes and loves his father so completely he agrees to take the sins of the world upon himself by living a life of perfect obedience and dying by execution on a cross. He is mocked and tortured by Roman soldiers. When the end comes he hangs dying in the hot sun, having been abandoned by most of the people dearest to him. Even the criminal hanging next to him heckles him (Luke 23).

In each instance single-minded obedience to what the Lord has spoken lends itself to the perception that each of these individuals is, in their turn, reckless.

The dangerous kind are recklessly obedient to the commands of the Lord. And inevitably, the world will see us as puzzling and sadly weak-minded. The Lord told his church early on that this is the way it would be. "God has chosen what the world calls foolish to shame the wise; he has chosen what the world calls weak to shame the strong," Paul writes, "He has chosen things of little strength and small repute, yes and even things which have no real existence to explode the pretensions of the things that are" (1 Corinthians 1:27-28 PHILLIPS). This lays bare that which renders us so incomprehensible to those who have yet to be apprehended by the love of God: we live in a realm that has no real existence to them. Little wonder, then, that they constantly try to persuade us to come down from the ledge of our hazardous belief system and rejoin them in the world of what can be known rationally and empirically. They enjoin us to live more sensibly on the basis of that which can be touched and seen and heard and smelled and known. They see our folly—aligning ourselves with invisible realities! *Really?*— and would welcome us back into the sensate universe where facts are established and truth can be verified in laboratories through accepted scientific methods. We are the objects of their pity and condescension, and our reckless obedience appears to them as little more plausible than the idea of riding a bike to the moon.

Reckless obedience to a God who propels us into invisible realities is fated to be perceived as outlandish. Even among the churched populace reckless obedience will not be universally applauded. Nominal, cautious followers of Christ who have been trained to excel at doing church as if it were the religious equivalent of the Rotary Club will regard such behavior as a bit over the top, as earnest but misguided and unhelpful when it comes to relating to the rest of the world.

The fact is that reckless obedience is not going to play very well on Main Street.

And, truth be told, those of us who commit ourselves to it may not like it very much, either.

Crazy Is as Crazy Does

Obedience to God's voice and a ready willingness to do all he requires are not guarantors of contentment or comfort. Quite often, in fact, when the Lord speaks, what he says doesn't just sound crazy to the rest of the world. It strikes us as crazy, too. The adventures of Jehoshaphat and Jehoram are illustrative.

The time is circa 845 BC. Solomon's kingdom is divided. The northern tribes, now known as Israel, are led by Jehoram. His father was the infamous Ahab, who with his wife Jezebel formed a Bonnie-and-Clyde-like, bloodletting, lawless royal tandem. Ahab is described as doing more evil and provoking God to greater anger than any king before him. Jehoram, the biblical archivist tells us, was "in God's sight, a bad king. But he wasn't as bad as his father and mother" (1 Kings 16:30, 33; 2 Kings 3:2 MSG). Faint praise for marginal improvement, for the apple had not fallen far from the tree.

The southern tribe is now known as Judah. Judah is ruled by Jehoshaphat, whose father Asa had followed hard after God. It is said that "Asa's heart was loyal to the Lord all his days." Jehoshaphat, who had established peace with the northern tribes, was not a perfect king (he failed to remove all the pagan shrines) but he was a good king. "He continued the kind of life characteristic of his father Asa—no detours, no dead ends—pleasing with his life" (1 Kings 15:14b; 1 Kings 22:43a MSG).

Theirs was an unlikely and not altogether stable alliance, born of necessity as both were surrounded by enemies committed to their total destruction. As we enter their story, they find themselves (along with the king of Edom) in a pickle because they have chosen to pursue a war against the Moabites without counting the cost or inquiring of the Lord. The enterprise can be traced to Jehoram's impulsive brashness and Jehoshaphat's charitable but unthinking response to his northern ally.

JEHORAM: *The king of Moab has rebelled against me, and I'm not going to stand for it. Let one of these vassals get away with it and the next thing you know, they're all thinking I'm fat and soft and easy pickings. I'm going to crush that worthless sheep breeder and teach everyone a lesson they won't forget. Will you help me?*

JEHOSHAPHAT: *Why, of course! I'm with you all the way. You and I are one; anyone who rebels against you rebels against me! My troops and horses are yours. What's the plan?*

Appetite for revenge runs in the family, and Jehoram determines to have his on the Moabites. He never pauses to consider whether or not going to war is a good idea, much less a noble one. All he can see is the insult to his honor, the injustice done to his reputation, and the injury to his royal coffers (King Mesha had been ponying up an annual tribute of 100,000 rams and 100,000 lambs). For his part, Jehoshaphat, overeager to preserve the peace with Israel he had worked so hard to win, promises aid without asking God if he should. Instead of inquiring of the Lord, "What would you have me do?" he declares his bond with Jehoram and asks, "What's the plan?"

The plan, as it turns out, isn't much of a plan at all.

Israel and Judah will attempt a backdoor sneak attack on Moab, making their route through the inhospitable wilderness of Edom. This indirect path may have looked like brilliant strategy on papyrus but it turned into catastrophe in the Edomite badlands. The armies of Israel and Judah walked and walked and walked. Seven days they walked. They walked until they were exhausted and there was no water left for men or animals.

Out of options, Jehoshaphat brightly volunteers, "Isn't there a prophet in our midst who can ask the Lord what we should do?" This would have been an excellent question to ask *before* setting off into a land with no water but plenty of snakes, jackals, and scorpions. Still, it's a savvy gambit by Jehoshaphat, who knows enough of Yahweh's ways to cry out to him when Judah's back is against the wall.

They go to Elisha, the personal assistant to Israel's most famous prophet at the time. Elisha makes no effort to hide his contempt for Jehoram, whom he regards as a spiritual whore unfit to occupy Israel's throne. But his respect for Jehoshaphat is so great that he prophesies as requested. And what he prophesies is an extraordinary reversal of fortune borne on the wings of God's miraculous intervention. As far as the eye can see there is only desolate, arid wilderness and sand. Sand to the left, to the right, behind them, in front of them. But, promises the prophet, God will move dramatically, and when he does water will fill the valley. It will be sudden and abundant, and it will signal Moab's defeat.

There's a catch, though.

Israel and Judah's weary, parched troops will be required to dig ditches. Lots and lots of ditches. This must be done under the unforgiving, relentless sun by men already so tired and dehydrated they can hardly stand upright. "Dig ditch after ditch," Elisha instructs them, "Don't stop until this valley is full of ditches. After you're done—and only after you've obeyed this edict from the Lord—your miracle will be upon you. You won't see storm clouds, you won't feel any winds, and rain will not fall from the sky. But as sure as the Lord Almighty lives, this dry land will be filled with pools of water" (2 Kings 3:16-17).

Israel and Judah have a decision to make: laugh off Elisha's instructions as mantic madness or offer the Lord reckless obedience. Reckless, because if they do what the prophet says and God does not show up, their troops will be reduced to the walking dead and Moab will surely route them. Reckless, because Elisha's command makes no sense to the natural mind. This is how the war shall be won, by digging ditch after ditch after ditch in the pitiless desert, by men who are so thirsty they are hallucinating oases? Only lunatics would agree to it. Even if, against all logic and expectation, water should subsequently come to the valley, it will refresh Israel and Judah's armies but it hardly ensures a victory against the rested forces of Moab.

No, this instruction makes no sense. Worse, it contradicts everything we know in the visible universe. If the prophet is wrong, it is suicide by stupidity.

Unless.

Unless God really said it and is going to back up his outrageous command with an even more outrageous response. Unless the God whose ways are not our ways and whose thoughts are higher than our thoughts is once again resorting to his preferred manner of invading this world: through a realm that has no real existence to those without spiritual eyes and through people and plans that great minds would dismiss as weak and foolish.

The Fellowship of Obedient Misery

It's hard to account for Jehoram's compliance with Elisha's counsel, given the king's syncretistic beliefs and practices. Even for a devotee of Yahweh like Jehoshaphat the requirement is bizarre and discouragingly burdensome. Nevertheless, both kings agree. And agreeing, they become God's ditch diggers. In so doing they join the fellowship of obedient misery. Often this is what reckless obedience brings us to: an immediate, deep misery in which we find ourselves in over our heads and wondering why we ever agreed to do what God said in the first place. There can be no doubt that the misery of Israel and Judah rises to unbearable levels as they perform their thankless task, digging ditches across the wadi with their thirst unslaked and their physical strength depleted.

Sometimes this is the way of it with God. He gives us instructions that run against the grain of common sense and when we obey, our misery increases. In this instance he tells men dying of thirst to dig holes in the desert. With Abraham it was a requirement to sacrifice the son he had waited for his entire adult life. He demands that Moses, who suffers from stage fright and is easily tongue-tied, to be his emissary to the world's most powerful ruler. He insists that Ananias befriend and offer healing prayer for blinded Saul of Tarsus, a man whose reputation for acts of barbarism against the new church is unrivalled. He tests Peter by inviting him to step out of a boat in gale force winds and walk on water. He tells a rich young man to sell all his possessions and give the money to the poor if he wants to be a Christ-follower.

The only option for people who want to be a threat to the designs of Satan and potent for the purposes of God is obedience. Reckless, misery-inducing, sacrificial, faith-filled obedience. Obedience that will be mystifying to a world that cannot see the unseen.

This is not how we would order the universe were the One who created it to consult us. He takes us to the end of our own resources and endurance before converting our reckless obedience into divine action. We want the blessings of God without breaking a sweat. We want obedience on our terms, and our terms are always highly favorable to us: little exertion, minimal discomfort, maximum and instant payout. It isn't going to be that way.

Fulfilling the inscrutable requirement of the Lord leads Israel and Judah to an improbable conquest of Moab. God's instruction for men who are staggering toward death to dig ditches in the desert is nonsensical, but they do it anyway because it is the will of the Lord. It is the word they are under. And as he always does when he has given his word, God comes through in a manner befitting his infinite imagination. "The next day at about the time when the morning sacrifice was offered, water suddenly appeared! It was flowing from the direction of Edom, and soon there was water everywhere" (2 Kings 3:20 NLT). The Moabites look out over the valley and mistake the water for blood. Believing the armies of Israel, Judah, and Edom have slaughtered each other, the Moabites rush in for the kill only to be ambushed and destroyed themselves. It is a military victory for Israel and Judah that would not have happened had they not heeded the Lord's directive. But they did. It was, in a word, reckless.

Reckless obedience makes God's people very, very dangerous. Oswald Chambers urges it upon all Christ-followers in his timeless devotional, *My Utmost for His Highest*. "If you debate for even one second when God has spoken, it is all over for you. Never start to say, 'Well, I wonder if He really did speak to me?' Be reckless immediately—totally unrestrained and willing to risk everything—by casting your all upon Him. You do not know when His voice will come to you, but whenever the realization of God comes, even in the faintest way imaginable, be determined to recklessly abandon yourself, surrendering everything to Him. It is only through abandonment of yourself and your circumstances that you will recognize Him. You will only recognize His voice more clearly through recklessness—being willing to risk your all."[61]

There's nothing easy about it. When God speaks it always has God-sized dimensions. When the Lord of the angel armies talks to us it will always be about something only God can do. We may balk when what he speaks looks like impossible, fantastic madness to us. This is often the point. He must take us beyond ourselves—beyond our skills, gifts, desires, and vision into the realm of his Spirit where what is unseen is truer than anything that can be

---

[61] Oswald Chambers, *My Utmost for His Highest: Updated Edition*, entry for June 18, James Reimann, ed. (Grand Rapids, MI: Discovery House Books; Oswald Chambers Publications Association, Ltd., 1995), n.p.

seen. All our lives we have been trained to believe that the natural world of the senses is the only real world, and certainly the only world to be trusted. When God speaks it is always to move us out of our world and into his. This is what makes reckless obedience so terrifying: we know if we take that step we will have to rely on God—throw the whole weight of our trust on him—to take care of us. In the parlance of Texas Hold 'Em, we will have to go *all in*, leaving no chips on the table and without a plan B. When God is on the move there is never a plan B and the players at the table don't have the option of holding a few chips in reserve. When God issues marching orders requiring reckless obedience, we will have to decide if God is really God and if he can be trusted when little to nothing of what he says makes sense to us. This is the nature of faith and the reckless obedience it inspires.

Obedience Begets Blessing

Obedience is evidence of our love for God. It's one thing to say we love God and another to prove it. The proof, as far as God is concerned, is found here: do we obey him? "The one who obeys me is the one who loves me," Jesus says (John 21:20 TLB). He's looking for people who will drop everything to follow him. He's looking to raise up a dangerous kind of disciple who will immediately and recklessly abandon everything and everyone for the privilege of knowing him and doing what he commands. Friends and acquaintances will urge caution upon us; moderation in all things, even spiritual things, is what they will commend. But there can be no measured approach to the measureless love of God.

For those who go all-in there is reward at the end of the road and, often, along the road as well. The Bible has much to say about the organic connection between obedience and blessing, between faithfulness and reward. We hesitate to affirm this connection, fearing we might give rise to a mindset of earning our blessings, a spiritual quid pro quo arrangement in which if we perform X, then God must deliver Y. This potential distortion of the biblical principle of blessing merits our alertness but we should not live in fear of it, nor should we fail to eagerly pursue the blessing God wants to give us. Well meaning teachers and preachers have warned us against seeking God's hand (blessing) instead of his face (presence), with the result that we have come away with the idea that it is unspiritual and inferior to desire blessing and pursue reward when what should really bring satisfaction is God alone, just him.

It is a spiritual-sounding but curious distortion. One cannot have God sans benefits. There is no blessing-free experience of God. The suggestion that he might impart something to us is not a warning shot across the bow to beware the infiltration of carnal motivation for obedience. If there is some higher, purer, freer obedience to God than that driven by our love for him, our fear of him, and our wish to receive his blessings, we're not capable of it. He wants to reward us and, presumably, he wants us to want what he wants for us. The idea that we shouldn't is absent in the Bible. To know God personally as father and friend is to be one to whom God imparts blessing after blessing and grace upon grace. He will have it—and us—no other way. The Jesus whom the dangerous kind follow *insists* on blessing and rewarding. It's who he is. It's what he's like. If we want something other than this then we want someone other than him.

When God blesses he does not bless slightly. He is not a tight-fisted father, reluctantly and parsimoniously handing out blessings in dribs and drabs. We want and need it to be true that our sacrificial, reckless following of him will have its reward. We are not the only ones. Peter pressed Jesus on the issue. "We've given up everything to follow you. What will we get?" Jesus' response is worth noting as much for what he does not say as what he does. Jesus doesn't reprimand Peter for wanting his discipleship to have a personal payoff. He doesn't lecture Peter about how unspiritual it is to want blessing from Jesus when being with Jesus is all the blessing anyone could possibly want or need. No, Jesus affirms the desire for reward and promises it is forthcoming in abundance for all who make the same choice as Peter. "I assure you that when the world is made new and the Son of Man sits upon his glorious throne, you who have been my followers will also sit on twelve thrones, judging the twelve tribes of Israel," he assures his headstrong friend. "And everyone who has given up houses or brothers or sisters or father or mother or children or property, for my sake, will receive a hundred times as much in return and will inherit eternal life" (Matthew 19:28-29 NLT).

Our God does not bless slightly. When we go to him for life, he does not mete it out churlishly but releases it joyfully and in excess. Jesus announces that in contrast to the devil, who brings death and destruction to all he touches, he has come to bring life in abundance. The word he uses in the original language, *perissos,* means "excessively, beyond, exceedingly, superabundantly." The Amplified Bible, which offers multiple English word equivalents for each key Hebrew and Greek word to assist the reader in understanding Scripture, translates the last portion of John 10:10, "I came that they may have and enjoy life, and have it in abundance (to the full, till it overflows)." *To the full, till it overflows*—this is what the armies of Israel and Judah experience after digging ditches in the desert. God doesn't bring just enough water to stave off dehydration. He *fills* the valley. There is water everywhere, as far as the eye can see. The water will save their lives. The water will bring about the unlikely defeat of their enemy. The water in its excessive superabundance is, above anything, an expression of God's love for his people.

Yet there is a paradox here. Blessings cannot be earned but they are connected to the requirement that we obey God when he speaks. The blessings we desire are freely given but they do not come without personal cost. Those who expect God's blessing must prepare room for it with their reckless obedience. Elijah's interaction with the widow of Zeraphath can be seen from this perspective. Both of them possess a crazy kind of faith and a willingness to do what God directs, even when what he asks is objectionable and offensive. Elijah's assignment appears deceptively simple: he must ask the widow for bread. What makes it hard is that he knows she is too poor even to feed herself. She and her son are on the brink of starvation; they have resigned themselves to one last meal, and then death. The prophet's request (1 Kings 17:10-11 MSG), "Please, would you bring me a little water in a jug? I need a drink. And while you're at it, would you bring me something to eat?" is a cruel one to make of an obviously impoverished woman. It is thoughtless and heartless, except that God is in the asking. Even so it must have tested Elijah to press this starving pauper to feed him when she cannot provide for herself or her boy. Only reckless obedience will move the question from his mind to his mouth.

The widow must offer an equally crazy obedience to the Lord: use the last of her meager provisions to feed the prophet first and then take the little that's left for a last supper for herself and her son. What would make her agree to such a thing? Faith, operating in the present tense, that the promise of the Lord through Elijah is true (1 Kings 17:14 NLT): if she'll obey, "there will always be flour and olive oil left in your containers until the time when the Lord sends rain and the crops grow again!"

Obedience begets blessing, and blessing requires that we empty our own resources so God can pour out his provision. It is a pattern set in Scripture and reflected in Elisha's ministry. In 2 Kings 4, he tells a woman who's down to her last flask of oil to borrow as many empty jars as she can from her friends and neighbors. Pouring olive oil from her tiny flask she is to fill them until there are no more containers to fill. How many receptacles should she gather? Well, how much blessing does she want? Likewise, Elisha tells Israel and Judah as they are on the edge of collapse and dying of thirst to fill the wadi with ditch after ditch after ditch. If they do this God will fill the valley with water and their desert will transform into a land of refreshing springs.

Partial obedience will not yield full blessing. The widow must do more than gather just a few jars; the soldiers cannot dig just enough ditches to get by. The widow must fill her house with jars and the soldiers the desert with ditches. Ever our flesh will ask when reckless obedience is required of us, "How many ditches should we dig?" Well, how much blessing do we want?

This is vastly different than "How much blessing do we deserve?" Because—and we know this, but it bears repeating—if it came down to deserving and getting accordingly, we would be miles away from blessing and in a universe of trouble. Everything that comes from God's hand is gift. None of what we receive from him results from any merit of our own. God gives lavishly and excessively according to his nature, not ours. God's blessings cannot be earned. Though they often follow obedience they do not come to us because we have performed at a sufficiently high level. They come to us out of the goodness of God's heart, from the overflow of his passion for abundance. They are never warranted by anything we have managed to achieve.

We are of two minds about this. Personally we are relieved that deserving is not God's litmus test for blessing. We know we are shockingly inconsistent in our walk with Christ, amateurs in this life of faith we feel we should have mastered by now. We sin and repent and vow not to go that way again only to find ourselves mired in absurd, self-defeating behaviors and darkened thought worlds. We are the ones Paul has in mind when he says, exasperated, "I'm completely frustrated by your unspiritual dealings with each other and with God. It's as though you are infants in Christ, not ready for anything stronger than milk, for you are still controlled by your sinful nature."[62] We've been caught out, and we know it, and we are genuinely thankful in these moments of honest self-assessment that our Father blesses and gives because it brings him pleasure. He gives for the joy of it. We don't deserve him or his benefits, and no matter how adept we become at following Jesus, we never will. From him cascade blessing upon grace upon gift, in spite of us and for the sake of us. We do not and cannot lay claim to his blessings on the basis of anything in us, and we are relieved at this.

---

[62] Compare 1 Corinthians 3:1-3 MSG and NLT.

We feel good about this for ourselves. How could we not? But privately we have some reservations about this arrangement when it comes to others. None of us deserve God's blessings, of course, but there are some people who *really* don't deserve them. God blesses them anyway. We do not approve.

This is how it works in the divine realm of our Father's life: God freely blesses the unworthy, even those who appear to be going all out to achieve record-setting sin lives. Jehoram is so evil the spokesman of Almighty God does not want to transmit God's blessing to him because, frankly, Elisha doesn't think Jehoram deserves it. "The stench of your spiritual treachery and idolatry make me want to vomit," Elisha tells him. "If it were up to me I'd let you and your kingdom perish right here in this hellhole of a desert."

This sentiment echoes frequently in the prayer book of the Bible. The psalmists are not shy about asking God to give renegade hearts and unrepentant pagans precisely what they deserve. "Lord," one pious prayer goes, "pay back our neighbors seven times for the scorn they have hurled at you!" Another urges God to "bring disgrace and destruction on my accusers. Humiliate and shame those who want to shame me." Still another cries out, "Please, Lord, rescue *me!* Come quickly, Lord, and help *me!*" But as for his enemies, the request is a little different: "Wipe their children from the face of the earth so they will never have descendants." There's nothing as satisfying as praying a holocaust on someone else, is there? But the psalmist is not finished. "A blessing on anyone," he says to his foes, "who seizes your babies and shatters them against a rock."[63]

Like Elisha, we resent that God showers blessings on sinful, self-important tyrants like Jehoram. We cannot fathom that he blesses blame-shifters, but he does. When he finds himself stranded in the wasteland with his army on its last legs, how does Jehoram explain this predicament? This way: it's all God's fault. Presumably he says it with a straight face. The king who perpetuates Jeroboam's sin of worshiping golden calves and who fails to consult the Lord before rashly setting out to make war against Moab has the temer-

---

[63] Psalm 79:12; 71:13; 40:13; 21:10; 137:9 (emphasis added).

ity to blame God. "Alas!" he cries out, "the Lord has brought the three of us here to let the king of Moab defeat us!" He's not kidding; he really believes it. He gets himself and his men into a jam with his reckless stupidity and his assessment is that God is to blame. Nothing new here, Proverbs tells us. "A man's own folly ruins his life, yet his heart rages against the Lord" (Proverbs 19:3 NIV). This, perhaps, is the most objectionable thing of all—God deliberately blesses this worthless blame-shifter! Not just slightly, either. Abundantly, filling the desert with pools of cool, sweet water and handing Jehoram's enemies over to him on a platter. The dangerous kind, who know all too well that we have blamed God for problems stemming from our own sinful, stupid, ill-conceived strategies, will not be too hard on Jehoram. We know that his story is ours too, and we are lucky to belong to a God who not only rewards reckless obedience but who also unreservedly blesses unworthy blame-shifters like us.

There's more good news. Not only does God bless sinners, he blesses the stupid. Jehoshaphat, the godly king in the ditch-digging drama, finds himself in this situation because when Jehoram asks for help he quickly assents. So quickly that God has no chance to get a word in. Jehoshaphat just does it, heedless of the consequences and absent of God's wisdom. The thing of it is, *he has done the exact same thing before!* A few years back, Ahab, Jehoram's despicable father, approached Judah's king with a proposal that the two kings join forces to go to war against the king of Aram. Jehoshaphat's answer a decade or so earlier is word for word the same answer he gives Ahab's son.[64] It was stupid then and it's stupid now. But it turns out that stupidity, while hardly a commendable character trait, is not an insuperable barrier to the release and reception of God's blessing. Nothing in all the world—including our sinful, blame-shifting, stupid ways—can shut down the blessing-obsessed heart of God.

---

[64] Compare 1 Kings 22:4 and 2 Kings 3:7.

Reckless Obedience Positions Us for the Unexpected

So what is it that prompts God's people to become God's ditch diggers? What impels the dangerous kind to offer a reckless obedience that leaves the world scratching its head? Faith born of love. Martin Luther memorably described faith as "a living, unshakeable confidence in God's grace; it is so certain that someone would die a thousand times for it. This kind of trust in and knowledge of God's grace makes a person joyful, confident, and happy with regard to God and all creatures. This is what the Holy Spirit does by faith. Faith is a work of God in us, which changes us and brings us to birth anew from God. It kills the old Adam, makes us completely different people in heart, mind, senses, and all our powers, and brings the Holy Spirit with it. What a living, creative, active, powerful thing is faith!"[65]

The old Adam would not give a second thought to reckless obedience because his first thought is always for himself, his happiness, and his comfort. Reckless obedience is automatically ruled out for the old Adam by virtue of its insistence on a higher reality and superior sacrifice. But when faith exerts itself the change it brings opens us to laying everything on the line for the sake of the One who laid everything on the line for us. When he speaks and commands us to acts of insane obedience, we answer the call. Not because we've had our spirituality supersized. And not because we are unmindful of the hot water such obedience might land us in. The old Adam is dead; the new Adam is answering. We obey because of faith, a daring resoluteness traceable to our belief that our Father can be trusted when he calls us out of the boat and onto the water, no matter how high the waves or wicked the winds.

This faith always operates in the present tense. It doesn't take much faith that God *did* mighty things back in the day, because

---

[65] Martin Luther, *Preface to the Letter of St. Paul to the Romans*, Andrew Thornton, trans., for the Saint Anselm College Humanities Program (Manchester, NH: Saint Anselm Abbey, 1983).

those things are already recorded. Nor does it take any faith to say that God *can* do mighty things, because God can do anything God wants to, and theoretically—who knows, we might get lucky—God may want to. It takes faith when God gives us a real opportunity, right now, to obey him when common sense tells us it would be crazy to do so.

At the heart of faith that births reckless obedience is real relationship with God. A deep, personal friendship with the God who scattered the stars down the backstreets of the cosmos will persuade us to act when rational thought argues against it. Because in this startlingly true companionship with God, the truest thing is what he says, and this trumps everything our senses tell us. When the invisible God calls us into invisible realities, we dare not resist on the basis of all the things we cannot see and do not know; we must obey on the basis of what we know about him.

What do we know about this God who shrouds himself in mystery, whose glory is so overwhelming Moses must hide in the crevice of a rock in order not to be struck dead when God passes by? What do we know about this God who inventories the storehouses of snow and cuts a path for thunderstorms? Quite a bit, as it turns out. We know he has plans to prosper us, not harm us. We know he loved us so crazily when we were at our absolute worst that he gave his absolute best to redeem us from death. We know he is faithful even when we are faithless. We know his love will pursue us to hell and back if that's what it takes to win us over. We know he is able to do above and beyond all we can ask or imagine. We know he sees the beginning from the end and causes all things to work together for good for those who love him and have been called according to his purpose. So we obey recklessly in faith and with a love we possess because he first loved us, knowing that no power on earth or in hell or in heaven can ever separate us from him.

Still, our obedience may not have a happy ending.

The blessings of obedience are many but this is not to infer that everything always works out in the end. Honesty requires this admission: sometimes when we obey, things get worse and go downhill from there. Hebrews 11 presents a roll call of recklessly obedient God-lovers, many of whom received heaven's promised blessings as a result. But there are some who did not and are still waiting. These people, truly dangerous followers of God, were tortured, beaten, imprisoned, mocked, and sawn in two. Some wandered from desert to cave to hole in the ground, homeless, unwanted, and destitute. For them there was no miracle rescue, no reversal of fortune, no last minute reprieve. Scripture doesn't offer any commentary, except to say that this world was not worthy of them. And now they assemble before the Lord in heaven and cry out from beneath the martyr's altar, "How long, Lord? How long before you avenge our blood and reward our obedience?"[66]

Whether in this age or in the age to come, God will make good on every promise and will reward every one of the dangerous kind who risked everything for him with astonishing, reckless obedience. Count on it. God always pays his bills.

When he does it is often in an unexpected fashion. When Jehoram and Jehoshaphat agree to become Yahweh's ditch diggers a most remarkable blessing ensues: Moab catches wind of the irresistible scent of easy victory and sweeps down into the valley to grab hold of it. But the destruction Moab perceives is a mirage— Israel and Judah are delivered by the Lord, Strong and True, and their deliverance is Moab's demise. This is characteristic of God's blessing; it counteracts the enemy's intention. Where the Devourer would bring devastation God's blessing brings bounty. As Joseph tells his brother who sold him into slavery, "As for you, you meant evil against me, but God meant it for good" (Genesis 50:20a ESV).

The dangerous kind who are committed to a daring confidence in God's grace must know this as they step out in reckless obedience. God will do it, but God will not do it the way we think. "Here's what will happen," God tells Israel and Judah as they are nearing their expiration date in the Edomite wilderness. "You won't hear the wind, you won't see the rain, but this valley is going to fill up with water." It takes place just as guaranteed. "The next

---

[66] Compare Hebrews 11:35-38 and Revelation 6:10.

morning, about the time for offering the sacrifice, there it was—water flowing from the direction of Edom! And the land was filled with water" (2 Kings 3:17a MSG; 3:20 NIV). No natural explanation, just supernatural action: water suddenly floods and overflows the desert. Where did it come from? How did it get there? Who can say? It should not surprise us. The rewards of God are often marked by the unpredictable suddenlies of God. We see it repeatedly in Scripture. The barrenness that sees us in exile and rejection is suddenly reversed and we find ourselves exclaiming, "Look at all these children! Where did they come from?" Our luckless attempt to bring in a great haul lasts all night until dropping our lines on the other side of the boat suddenly brings a catch that strains our nets. Our devotion to Jesus leads us into lonely imprisonment when suddenly the angel of the Lord appears and leads us to our liberty. One day in the future, God will move, and suddenly the martyrs will be avenged and rewarded, and God's justice set loose upon this dark world. Just like he said.

It's really true. God always pays his bills.

Now, we cannot assume he will do it for us the way he did it for someone else. This means the dangerous kind, the mighty ones of God, must constantly keep fellowship with him. Here, in the heart of the One whose heart alone is true and faithful, the dangerous kind will find themselves delighted and amazed at how God accomplishes his purposes and performs his Word and pays his bills.

This Is the Key to Your Life

In the Best Picture of 1972, *The Godfather*, Michael Corleone describes to his girlfriend, Kay, how his father helped a popular singer get out of an ironclad contract with a big-band leader. The band leader adamantly resisted letting Johnny Fontaine out of his contract, but the Godfather persuaded him to do so for a mere thousand dollars.

"How did he do that?" Kay marvels.

"My father made him an offer he couldn't refuse."

Our Father in heaven is doing the same thing. He's making us an offer we can't refuse. In life, as in the film, there are two choices. For the band leader, the choice was stark. "Luca Brasi held a gun to his head," Michael tells Kay, "and my father assured him that either his brains or his signature would be on the contract."[67] It was life or death. The band leader had a choice but no true alternative. The Godfather had made him an offer he couldn't refuse.

The choice before us is life and death. There is no hulking mobster holding a gun to our head, but the stakes are equally ultimate. They are the same stakes facing the Israelites when they are told they

---

[67] *The Godfather*, Francis Ford Coppola, director, written by Mario Puzo and Francis Ford Coppola (Paramount Pictures, 1972). Based on the novel by Mario Puzo.

must make a decision about their future. "Today I have given you the choice between life and death, between blessings and curses," Moses announces.

> Now I call on heaven and earth to witness the choice you make. Oh, that you would choose life, so that you and your descendants might live! You can make this choice by loving the Lord your God, obeying him, and committing yourself firmly to him. This is the key to your life. And if you love and obey the Lord, you will live long in the land the Lord swore to give your ancestors Abraham, Isaac, and Jacob (Deuteronomy 30:19-20 NLT).

This is how the Lord makes us an offer we can't refuse. Not with a gun to the head but with an invitation to the heart. He places before us life and death and pleads with us to choose him and all that life with him includes. We hear his entreaties throughout the pages of Scripture, from the opening story to the closing crescendo. In the middle of the Garden of Eden stood the tree of the knowledge of good and evil. "And the Lord God commanded the man, 'You are free to eat from any tree in the garden; but you must not eat from the tree of the knowledge of good and evil, for when you eat of it you will surely die'" (Genesis 2:16-17 NIV). We can hear in the Father's voice as he makes an offer Adam cannot refuse the passionate plea of Moses 2,500 years later: *"Oh, that you would choose life so that you and your descendants might live!"* As we come to the Bible's final chapter we discover that God's appeal has not changed. "The Spirit and the bride say, 'Come!' And let him who hears say, 'Come!' Whoever is thirsty, let him come; and whoever wishes, let him take the free gift of the water of life" (Revelation 22:17 NIV).

Our Father makes us an offer we cannot refuse.

But we do. We always have.

The garden is a sobering reminder of humanity's penchant for self-destruction. The first man and first woman are made an offer no one in their right mind would refuse: "You may live in paradise, enjoying every aspect of its bounty, provided you do not eat from one tree in particular. But every other tree, plant, animal is yours for the taking. Only one is off limits. If you harvest it and eat its fruit, you will surely die." We know the story. We remember it without effort because although Adam and Eve are the actors in the drama, the story is timeless and has been reenacted in every generation. God made Adam and Eve an offer they couldn't refuse. Adam and Eve refused it anyway. Since that time all of their children have reprised their role, rehearsed their rebellion, and repeated their refusal.

Again and again when the choice is between life and death humans stubbornly insist on death. The One least surprised by this is the One who made us, loves us, and refuses to stop pursuing us. After Moses catalogues the consequences of obedience (blessing) and disobedience (curses) for Israel, God takes his friend aside and confides in him. Speaking from a pillar of cloud over the Tent of Meeting the Lord tells him, "You're about to die and be buried with your ancestors. You'll no sooner be in the grave than this people will be up and whoring after the foreign gods of this country that they are entering. They will abandon me and violate my Covenant that I've made with them" (Deuteronomy 31:16 MSG). Perhaps this is why the first thing God says to Moses' appointed successor, Joshua, is, "Be strong and courageous" (Deuteronomy 32:23 NIV). He'll need to be, given how pigheaded the Israelites are and how difficult they will make his job. So the Lord reiterates his instruction to Joshua three times in the span of nine verses, the last time giving it special emphasis. "Have I not commanded you? Be strong and courageous. Do not be terrified; do not be discouraged, for the Lord your God will be with you wherever you go" (Joshua 1:9 NIV).

"Paradise or punishment—you choose," God says.

"Heaven or Hell—your choice," God says.

"Blessing or curses—your decision," God says.

Our God-Father makes this offer repeatedly. It is, seemingly, an offer we couldn't refuse.

Joshua, schooled by the greatest leader in Israel's history, lays out the same invitation for the people as his predecessor. "Serve the Lord alone. But if you refuse to serve the Lord, then choose today whom you will serve. Would you prefer the gods your ancestors served beyond the Euphrates? Or will it be the gods of the Amorites in whose land you now live? But as for me and my family, we will serve the Lord" (Joshua 24:14b-15 NLT).

Life On the Narrow Way

The categories are fixed in this offer we cannot but all too often do refuse: the God life and the not-God life. James lays it out for his congregation in terms every bit as sobering as those of God in Eden, Moses in the wilderness, and Joshua in the Promised Land: "Do you not know that being the world's friend is being God's enemy? So whoever chooses to be a friend of the world takes his stand as an enemy of God" (James 4:4b AMP).

The choice before the dangerous kind is explicit: the narrow way of the kingdom versus the sixteen-lane superhighway of the world, a superior but inestimably more hazardous life versus an inferior but less personally demanding life. The narrow way is the way of Jesus' own ministry, doing what he did in radical dependence on the Holy Spirit and stirring up all manner of spiritual reprisals as a result. The narrow way is the commitment to remember the poor and to incarnate the kindness of heaven's king to the forgotten ones of our society. The narrow path disdains the spotlight and embraces being hidden in Christ's life. It places itself under the Word, not over it, and submits quickly to its demands, constraints, and requirements. The narrow way is the heart-healing road of repentance, reckless obedience, and love as the absolute gold standard of kingdom life. The narrow way is the only road open to the dangerous kind, who have been made this offer by their Father: you can have life to the full, 'til it overflows. Or you can have the pseudo life of nominal Christianity in which the world will ever serve you tea as you spend your days in pursuits that never fully engage you.

The choice is real and it is before each person who names Jesus of Nazareth as Lord. This One whom we claim as our own makes this claim upon us (Matthew 7:13-14 PHILLIPS): "Go in by the narrow gate. For the wide gate has a broad road which leads to disaster and there are many people going that way. The narrow gate and the hard road lead out into life and only a few are finding it." Making the right choice, the dangerous choice, is everything.

> *Two roads diverged in a wood, and I –*
> *I took the one less travelled by,*
> *And that has made all the difference.*[68]

He was not commenting on the Christian life, but Robert Frost nonetheless expertly summarizes the stakes. Choosing the right road makes all the difference.

Just here we must be careful not to commit a fundamental error: believing that the choice has essentially to do with behavior and beliefs, with performing certain tasks or adopting a better and truer portfolio of doctrines. Behaviors, tasks, doctrines—all will factor into the kingdom life of the dangerous kind but they are not the central point.

The central reality is Jesus. The narrow way is Jesus himself; it is not a road we take that leads us toward kingdom reality. The road, the way, the gate—it is Jesus. He is kingdom reality and the core of dangerous living. Friendship with him, unconditional submission to him, non-negotiable commitment to him—this is the way of the dangerous kind. Every other way, any other way, is a lesser way. His way is only ever all-in, a risk-taking way that looks illogical to rhetoricians, extreme to professional churchmen, and like madness to the uninvested occupant of the pew.

---

[68] Robert Frost, "The Road Not Taken," in *The Norton Anthology of Modern Poetry,* Richard Ellmann and Robert O'Clair, eds. (New York: W. W. Norton & Company, 1973), 197.

The Jesus who is the way of the dangerous kind and the road less traveled by is not the quiescent face of niceness, the poster boy for harmless comportment, good manners, and modest religious accomplishment. The Jesus who is the way is the teacher who cleared the classroom with a distasteful message about eating his flesh and drinking his blood as the way to living forever, without the courtesy of indicating he was speaking in metaphors. He's the dinner guest who leaves his host aghast and fellow invitees wondering how he managed to crash their comfortable party. He turns over tables and takes braided whips to the religious elite and their cherished spiritual sensibilities. He elicits consternation and disapproval everywhere he goes. He could hardly care less about public opinion. He could hardly care less that he constantly offends, horrifies, disturbs, upends, jolts, mystifies, baffles, and perplexes. The things most of us care most about he could hardly care less about.

But he could hardly care more for the broken, for the unesteemed, for the losers and low lifes, for the down-and-out deadbeats and has-beens and never-weres. He could hardly care more for the prisoners, the demonized, the disadvantaged, the invisible men and women exiled to the fringes of our social order. He could hardly care more for those worn down by a world indifferent to and inconvenienced by their existence. He could hardly care more for those beaten up and slapped around by the religious zealots and spiritual despots of their day.

This is the Jesus who is the way. It is the way we walk when we walk with him. And so his offer comes to all who have ears to hear: "I'm looking for people who could hardly care less. I'm looking for people who could hardly care more. I'm looking for someone, anyone, willing to be the dangerous kind."

It is an offer we cannot refuse.

If only it were that easy.

But it never is.

It Is Never Easy

It is never easy for us because it was never easy for him. So he alerts those who would eagerly sign on the dotted line to become the dangerous kind, "Not so fast. Let's be clear about this: sign up with me and you sign your life away. You will be arrested, persecuted, and killed. You will be hated all over the world because you are my followers. And when the world hates you, know this: it hated me before it ever hated you."[69] This is the word the dangerous kind are under. It is not a temporary word. It is an all-time word for people who have thrown in their lot with and thrown away their lives on Jesus. It is never easy to say yes to this offer we cannot refuse.

It's never easy because the one who opposed him opposes us. The one who attempted to lure Jesus away from real life with the glittering treasures of pseudo life vigilantly places the same temptations before Jesus' followers. He failed with Jesus but his success rate among Jesus' friends is unnerving. The one who incited the crowds to turn against Jesus and motivated religious watchdogs to push for his execution is the same one who plots our downfall and demise. This is the one who would stand in our way—the way of the Christ—and barricade it with all his devices. He isn't lazy, he never stops, and he never sleeps. He is reminiscent of Hollywood's Terminator, a killing machine sent back in time to assassinate the woman who will give birth to humanity's savior. "You still don't get it, do you?" Kyle Reese bellows at a condescending psychiatrist who doesn't believe the Terminator exists. "He'll find her! That's what he does! That's *all* he does! You can't stop him. He'll wade through you, reach down her throat, and pull her heart out."[70]

This scene from James Cameron's film is a suitable summary of Lucifer's designs. He'll find us. That's what he does. That's *all* he does. We can't stop him in our own power, and if we try he will

---

[69] Compare Matthew 24:9 and John 15:18.

[70] *The Terminator*, James Cameron, director, written by James Cameron and Gale Ann Hurd with acknowledgement to the works of Harlan Ellison; additional dialogue by William Wisher, Jr. (Orion Pictures, 1984). This quote adapted (expletive deleted).

wade through us, reach down our throat, and pull our heart out. He's ruthless, tricky, violent, and relentless. He disguises himself as an angel of light so he can catch us off guard. He comes at us from every angle. Jesus does not take him lightly, not for a moment. Therefore he warns his followers that Satan was "a murderer from the beginning, not holding to the truth, for there is no truth in him. When he lies, he speaks his native language, for he is a liar and the father of lies." Hell's gatekeeper is wily enough to plague the apostle Paul and hinder Paul's ministry plans. Jesus says Satan is so slippery that at the end of the age the devil will unleash false Jesuses upon the world who can do jaw-dropping signs and wonders, even deceiving the elect.[71]

This one stands in the way of all those who would travel the Jesus way; he would cut off the dangerous kind before they have the chance to become dangerous. The father of lies urges us to settle for nominal Christianity, for an unobtrusive, inoffensive fondness for Jesus that sentimentalizes him and minimizes the kingdom reign he ushers in. It is Satan who sidles up next to us and whispers dark encouragement to settle for a lesser life than the King of Life came to make available. He invites us to make ourselves comfortable beneficiaries of God's grace but never agents of it. He tells us that the idea that we are to imitate and walk in Christ's supernatural ministry is mythology for half-wits. He's the one who sells us on the philosophy that since we will always have the poor with us—these are Jesus' words, and his Father's, after all (Mark 14:7a; Deuteronomy 15:11a)—then it is senseless to attempt to do anything about poverty. It's Lucifer's smooth dissembling we hear when it occurs to us that if God has promised his people they will be the head and not the tail, destined for the top and not the bottom—this is Scripture, remember (Deuteronomy 28:13)—then we ought to grasp for promotion and greatness as our divine prerogative, realizing that obscurity and hiddenness are the portion of the losers and luckless among us. It is Lucifer's seduction to believe that our words, thoughts, and judgments trump God's Word, and that

---

[71] See 2 Corinthians 11:14, John 8:44, 1 Thessalonians 2:18, and Mark 13:22, respectively.

we are free to pick and choose the words of God we like and discard the ones we deem personally irrelevant or culturally insensitive. Satan makes a play for our heart, easily deceived and desensitized as it is, and assures us love must be doled out in careful measure to those meriting it but never to those who do not. How awful it would be, he tells us, to love someone who engages in practices and promotes viewpoints we do not, and in so doing inadvertently endorse them and their flawed, sinful ways. Keep love in reserve and guard your heart, the thief of hearts counsels us; it is much smarter and safer that way. *Not* loving unconditionally—that's really better for everyone concerned. Apollyon, angel of the bottomless pit, fouls the good life with advice from the sewer of his darkness. He denigrates love and promotes the anti-God propaganda that repentance is an outmoded notion steeped in shame over things that men and women of modernity have learned to accept and embrace as perfectly natural.

This is the way it plays out, the way it has always played out in this life. When God our Father makes us an offer we cannot refuse, the Antichrist is prepared to act as our Consigliore. He will flood every manner of deceit into our spirit; his purpose is uncomplicated: he comes to destroy the children of the light, that they might never become dangerous. But we are not defenseless. "And I will ask the Father, and he will give you another Counselor to be with you forever—the Spirit of truth," Jesus reassures us. "The world cannot accept him, because it neither sees him nor knows him. But you know him, for he lives with you and will be in you. I will not leave you as orphans; I will come to you" (John 14:16-18 NIV).

Heaven's Counselor is the genuine article, a voice to be trusted against the advent of hell's counterfeiter. The Holy Spirit is introduced by Jesus to his disciples as their personal advocate, an encourager who can be relied upon to lead into all truth. The enemy trucks in lies but the Spirit moves in truth exclusively, exposing the devil's forgeries and frauds so that God's friends can move easily and in natural rhythm with God's grace. The Holy Spirit triggers landslides of the Father's love into our hearts and a confidence that any offer our Father makes is always supremely good. Ever will the enemy whisper, "Did God really say?" and ever will the Holy Spirit bring assurance of the truth, recalling to our minds and commending to our hearts all that Jesus has said. When we falter along the way, falling into sin because we have been seduced by the falsehoods of that trickster fox, it is the Holy Spirit who certifies that our failure is not fatal.

The devil, never content with initiating rebellion and wrongdoing, will argue against the gift of mercy. He will shame us and scold us and scare us, insisting that our bad behavior condemns us before all the angels and that our failings are the final word on our lives. "You had your chance," he'll tell us when God makes us an offer to become the dangerous kind and we refuse it, "You blew it. And that's all there is to say—you're done for." Then Lucifer will use the word of God against us, declaring our destiny arrested on the basis of our Father's own statements: "Because you would not listen to the Lord your God, the Lord will find pleasure in destroying you. The Lord will cause your heart to tremble, your eyesight to fail, and your soul to despair. Your life will constantly hang in the balance. You will live night and day in fear, unsure if you will survive. For you will be terrified by the awful horrors you see around you" (Deuteronomy 28:62b, 63a, 65b, 66, 67b NLT). Cue the music from *Jaws*, for the Great White shark of our sins is approaching at terrible speed and with a terrible appetite to feast on our failure, leaving us abandoned, broken, and bleeding in waters too wide to cross over.

The enemy will assure us of our abandonment, employing the words of Jesus to prove the trouble we've made for ourselves by rejecting God's offer will be our undoing. Not only that, it will be our own fault. "How often would I have gathered your children together as a mother fowl gathers her brood under her wings, *and you refused!*" Jesus says to the Jerusalemites who rejected him, "Behold, your house is forsaken and desolate (abandoned and left destitute of God's help). For I declare to you, *you will not see Me again.*"[72] So the

---

[72] Matthew 23:37b-39a AMP (emphasis added).

death-whisperer strikes down those who would be dangerous by calling into testimony against them the words of their sacred text and sacred Lord.

At this point, left to ourselves, our hearts would fail us.

Headline from the Home Front: God Is Greater than Our Hearts

But we are not left alone. At the Son's express request the Father has sent us an Ally. He comes to us himself, having promised never to forsake or abandon us. He comes as Helper, knowing the wreck we've made of things and foreseeing that we will do it again and again in the future. For God, our plight and the promise of our possibilities are personal. So he does not send us help, as though it were a commodity. He sends us himself. He is Help personified and so he comes just as the psalmist describes (Psalm 40:17 ESV). "You are my help and my deliverer!" He is the antidote for the poison of our enemy's accusations. Satan employs God's Word against us; it is one of his favorite tactics. With this device he tells us the truth, as God's Word can never be a lie. Indeed, Satan tells us the truth, but only some of it. He gives us a part of the Word, withholding the portion that would give us hope of a future with the One who promises to make us dangerous.

This is one of the central reasons the Holy Spirit is given to us. Satan will lead us into some of the truth; the Holy Spirit will lead us into all of it. Half truth is like half a life—it is no truth, no life at all. Jesus comes with excessive, overflowing, over-the-top life as the One who is Truth, and the Holy Spirit always leads us back to him. When we sin Satan immediately moves in for the kill, convincing us that it's all over for us. The Holy Spirit moves with even greater agility and alacrity to remind us that God's activity from the beginning of time to the end is one of patient, insistent restoration. It is the Father's primary project and he will never abandon it, or us. This is why God's announcement of punishment and consequences for disobedience are always followed by promises of healing and resurrection when we return to him. Nehemiah marvels at the unstoppable kindness of God in the face of Israel's addiction to sin (Nehemiah 9:28 NLT). "But as soon as they were at peace, your people again committed evil in your sight, and once more you let their enemies conquer them. Yet whenever your people turned and cried to you again for help, you listened once more from heaven. In your wonderful mercy, you rescued them many times!" Scripture's witness is consistent: humans sin, even when they have every reason not to, and their sin has real consequences. But this is not the whole truth, as though the story ends there. We are, in the words of the classic hymn, "prone to wander, prone to leave the God I love," but there has never been a prodigal who could outrun the Father's love. So Moses spoke this assurance to a nation prone to prodigalism: "Should you have been banished to the very sky's end, Yahweh your God will gather you again even from there, will come there to reclaim you" (Deuteronomy 30:4 NJB).

This is truth that blows prison doors right off their hinges. Whenever our hearts condemn us, God is greater than our hearts. Whenever our sin accuses us, God is greater than our sin. When it comes to being the dangerous kind, even though we keep refusing, God keeps offering. Why? Can't he take a hint? Can't he take no for an answer? Well, yes, he can, but he'd really rather not. He knows us better than we could ever hope to know ourselves. Our sin and stubbornness never surprise him and they do not deter him. He knows what we can be if only we will say yes to him. He knows what lies ahead for us if only we will agree with him and take hold of it. "For I know the thoughts that I think toward you, says the Lord, thoughts of peace and not of evil, to give you a future and a hope" (Jeremiah 29:11 NKJV).

This is his declaration to those whom he invites into a dangerous life with him. Be sure of this: Satan will attempt to defeat us before we can get started by pointing out our limitations and failings and sinfulness. He'll remind us of every promise we've ever made and broken to God and tell us this commitment to be the dangerous kind is no different. He'll remind us how temporary our commitment has been in the past and how often our best intentions have resulted in mediocre outcomes. He'll tell us how laughable it is to imagine we could be potent for the kingdom when we cannot get elementary sinful impulses under control. He'll laugh at us, the devil will, loud and long at the fantastic notion that we might amount to anything for God, that we might become people who change the odds just by showing up because when we show up God shows up. This is what our adversary does; this is who he is: a belittling dream-thief who snuffs out hope and cancels destiny. Our God-Father makes us an offer we cannot refuse, and the tormentor of our soul scoffs.

But the One enthroned in heaven laughs louder. Because he knows. He knows us, what he has placed of himself in us, and what extraordinary lives we will lead if we welcome him. He knows our weaknesses and vulnerabilities, and he knows his power manifests itself more magnificently in this environment than any other. He knows we can do it, knows we can truly become the dangerous kind, because there is nothing he cannot do in a life that is whole-heartedly submitted to him. He knows the best about us when we are at our worst, and he knows the best is yet to come in and through us. He knows the beauty he wove into us while we were in our mother's womb, the life-words he pronounced over us before we were born, the creation-shaping possibilities of each child bearing his image.

Yes, the One enthroned in heaven laughs louder. Because he knows. He knows how scared our enemy is, how nervous Satan is that we will learn the truth about ourselves, how worried he is that we will find out the offer God makes to become the dangerous kind is for real, that *we* are for real when we walk with the One who made us. God knows our accuser is a world-class con artist whose great fear is that we will discover he's been running a game on us we do not have to play. The One enthroned in heaven laughs because he knows our opponent is a poseur and a grifter who cannot withstand the light, and that for all our sad forays into the shadow lands and dark valleys of sin, we are light bearers and darkness breakers. We are light, the thing hells fears most and is powerless against. Light-bearing, light-carrying, light-igniting, light-releasing—these are the marks of the dangerous kind. That's why when we arrive on the scene demons tremble and rage, because when the dangerous kind come they come as destroyers of the darkness. When the dangerous kind show up the gospel is proclaimed to the poor, captives are broken out of prison, the blind gain sight, the oppressed are lifted up and lifted out, the favor of the Lord is free-flowing. When we say yes to the offer we cannot refuse we become inalterably, terrifyingly dangerous.

This is true, and heaven knows it. Hell knows it, too, which is why the warfare we face is so intense. Hell doesn't mind cookie-cutter religiosity, religious people doing their religious things. Hell isn't threatened by benign neighborhood churches holding bake sales. Hell isn't unnerved by mega-churches pursuing a bigger piece of the pie, Christian television jockeying for greater market share, or the latest Christian celebrity grasping for heightened visibility. None of these register so much as a blip on hell's radar screen. But hell is understandably troubled by the possibility that when we hear the Father's offer, we will say yes and enter the life the Father prepared for us before creation.

Does becoming the dangerous kind matter? As Moses told Israel when laying out the blessings of obedience and the curses of disobedience, *this is the key to your life*. It is an invitation to live far beyond the tempered aspirations of institutionalized religious life, where the highest and best we can hope for are modifications in our behavior, membership in a local church, and a memorialized connection to Jesus in which we remember who he was and what he did for us two millennia ago. The Father's offer catapults us into the ongoing, unfolding ministry of Jesus and the fulfillment of his promise that we will do even greater things than he did; it obliterates niceness as a Christian value and establishes reckless, perilous following of Jesus as an assumed non-negotiable. Responding to the Father's offer transports us from low impact Christianity to high octane kingdom living. No wonder our enemy the devil prowls around like a roaring lion, looking for some victim to devour! No wonder God says to us as he extends his improbable invitation to become dangerous, *"This is the key to your life."*

What we do and say in response matters. It matters in heaven, it matters in hell, and perhaps most crucially, it matters on earth. Becoming dangerous changes the atmosphere, and what's in the air matters.

All I Wanted Was a Haircut

I once knew a woman who remained baffled, years later, at how she ended up becoming a Christ-follower. When I asked her about her faith story, she was a bit overwhelmed as she searched her memory. She couldn't seem to find the words to adequately describe her surprise that she ever became a disciple of Mary's son. So she just sat there wordlessly, lost in a private world of reverie.

"How did you come to know Jesus?" I prompted her gently.

"I don't really know," she stammered. "All I remember is that one day I went out to get my hair done, and I came home a Christian."

Her eyes grew misty. "All I wanted was a haircut."

All she wanted was a haircut. What she got was eternal life. Now *that's* a dangerous hairdresser.

When God puts his offer of dangerous living on the table, the choice we make is vitally important. It carries the weight of Israel's answer to Joshua's challenge to choose which god they will serve. When, as Israel did, we say yes, we stand in line for the same somber admonishment they received from Joshua.

"You are accountable for this decision," Joshua said. "You have chosen to serve the Lord."

"Yes," they replied, "we are accountable."

"All right then," Joshua said (Joshua 24:22-23a NLT, 1st ed.).

When we answer the call to authentic life in Christ the conversation is much the same.

"You are accountable for this decision," the Holy Spirit says. "You have chosen to become the dangerous kind."

"Yes," we reply, "we are accountable."

"All right then," the Lord says.

All right then. Let's get busy dying so we can get busy living. Let's trust him to perform his word through absolute beginners and bumbling amateurs like us. Let's believe the life and love of God can so saturate us that when we show up, he shows up with mercy, encouragement, power, goodness, grace, and healing in his wings.

It's time for the world to stop serving us tea.

It's time to move from fuzzy sentimentality to radical friendship with Jesus.

It's time to trade an inferior existence of modest ambition for a superior life of maximum adventure.

It's time to say yes to the Father's summons to become the dangerous kind.

This is the key to your life.

Sources

Books:

Barrett, David B. and Todd M. Johnson. *World Christian Trends AD 30-AD 2000: Interpreting the Annual Christian Megacensus*. Pasadena, CA: William Carey Library, 2001.

Barth, Karl. *Church Dogmatics*, IV/3. G. W. Bromiley, trans. Edinburgh, Scotland: T & T Clark, 1975.

Bonhoeffer, Dietrich. *Life Together: The Classic Exploration of Christian Community*. New York: Harper and Row, 1954.

Chambers, Oswald. *My Utmost for His Highest: Updated Edition*, entry for June 18. James Reimann, ed. Grand Rapids, MI: Discovery House Books; Oswald Chambers Publications Association, Ltd., 1995.

Chavda, Mahesh. *The Hidden Power of Prayer and Fasting*. Shippensburg, PA: Destiny Image, 1998.

Cullman, O. *Christ and Time: The Primitive Christian Conception of Time and History*. F. V. Filson, trans. London: SCM Press, Ltd., 1951.

Cummings, E. E. *Complete Poems 1913-1962*. New York: Harcourt Brace Jovanovich, 1980.

Forde, Gerhard O. *Where God Meets Man*. Minneapolis, MN: Augsburg Publishing House, 1972.

Frost, Robert. "The Road Not Taken." In *The Norton Anthology of Modern Poetry*. Richard Ellmann and Robert O'Clair, eds. New York: W. W. Norton & Company, 1973.

Günther, Walther. *The New International Dictionary of New Testament Theology*, Vol. 1. Grand Rapids, MI: Zondervan Publishing House, 1975

Kearns Goodwin, Doris. *Team of Rivals: The Political Genius of Abraham Lincoln*. New York: Simon & Schuster, 2005.

Lewis, C. S. *The Last Battle*. New York: Macmillan, 1970.

Lewis, C. S. *The Screwtape Letters*. New York: Macmillan, 1962.

Luther, Martin. *Preface to the Letter of St. Paul to the Romans*. Andrew Thornton, trans., for the Saint Anselm College Humanities Program. Manchester, NH: Saint Anselm Abbey, 1983.

Miller, Donald. *Searching for God Knows What*. Nashville, TN: Thomas Nelson, 2004.

Nee, Watchman. *Sit, Walk, Stand*. Wheaton, IL: Tyndale House Publishers, 1977.

Osborne, Charles. *W. H. Auden: The Life of a Poet*. New York: M. Evans and Company, 1979.

Packer, J. I. *Affirming the Apostles' Creed*. Wheaton, IL: Crossway Books, 2008.

Pinnock, Clark. *Flame of Love: A Theology of the Holy Spirit.* Downers Grove, IL: InterVarsity Press, 1996.

Piper, John. *The Future of Justification.* Wheaton, IL: Crossway Books, 2007.

Yancy, Phillip. *Prayer—Does It Make Any Difference?* Grand Rapids, MI: Zondervan, 2006.

E-Content (Websites and Software):

Barclay, William. The summary of Paul's charge. In *The Daily Study Bible.* WORDsearch 9 Bible software, build 9.0.2.125.

Blesse, Barbara. "The Solemnity of the Most Holy Trinity." June 3, 2007. http://learn.ctu.edu.

Calvin, John. *Commentary on 1 Peter.* WORDsearch 9 Bible software, build 9.0.2.125.

Gibson, Teresa. *e. e. cummings' 'Daughters of the Church' as St. Paul's 'tinkling cymbals.'* http://blue.utb.edu.

"Kim Peak." Wikipedia. http://en.wikipedia.org/wiki/Kim_Peek.

"Koyaanisqatsi (complete original soundtrack)." Phillip Glass. http://www.philipglass.com/music/recordings/Koyaanisqatsi-09. php.

MacDonald, George. "The New Name." *Unspoken Sermons.* The Literature Network. http://www.online-literature.com/ george-macdonald/unspoken-sermons/5/.

Merriam Webster Online Dictionary. http://www.merriam-webster. com/dictionary/under.

Paton, Bruce C. "Cold, Casualties, and Conquests: The Effects of Cold on Warfare." In *Medical Aspects of Harsh Environments*, Vol. 1. U.S. Army Medical Department, The Borden Institute. http:// www.bordeninstitute.army.mil/published_volumes/harshEnv1/ harshenv1.html.

Quinn, Sally. "In Washington, That Letdown Feeling." *The Washington Post.* November 2, 1998. http://www.washingtonpost. com.

Robertson, A. T. *Robertson's Word Pictures in the New Testament*, Matthew 16:17. WORDsearch 9 Bible software, build 9.0.2.125.

Spurgeon, C. H. *Faith's Checkbook.* Devotional for April 18. http://www.lightsource.com/devotionals/faiths-checkbook-by-ch-spurgeon/faiths-checkbook-april-18-11538361-11538361.html.

Storm, Sam. "Defeat of Devil-Demons." Enjoying God Ministries. November 8, 2006. http://enjoy.monkcms.net.

Thiefe, Chris. "Ritual Human Sacrifice in the Bible." www. evilbible.com/Ritual_Human_Sacrifice.htm.

"Torah through Time." Story Tour. http://projectshalom2.org/ StoryTour/?p=117.

Webster's New World College Dictionary. Cleveland, OH: Wiley Publishing, Inc. http://www.yourdictionary.com/under.

Movies:

Annie Hall, Woody Allen, director. Written by Woody Allen and Marshall Brickman. United Artists, 1977.

Babe. Chris Noonan, director. Adapted from the novel *Babe: The Gallant Pig* by Dick King-Smith. Universal Studios, 1995.

Furious Love. Darren Wilson, writer, director. Wanderlust Productions, 2010.

The Godfather. Francis Ford Coppola, director. Written by Mario Puzo and Francis Ford Coppola. Based on the novel by Mario Puzo. Paramount Pictures, 1972.

The Lord of the Rings, The Two Towers. Peter Jackson, director. Based on the novel by J. R. R. Tolkien. New Line Cinema, 2002.

Star Wars Episode IV: A New Hope. George Lucas, writer, director. 20th Century Fox, 1977.

The Terminator. James Cameron, director. Written by James Cameron and Gale Ann Hurd with acknowledgement to the works of Harlan Ellison; additional dialogue by William Wisher, Jr. Orion Pictures, 1984.

Scripture references

New Testament scripture quotations marked "AMP" are taken from *The Amplified Bible*, New Testament. Copyright © 1954, 1958, 1987, by The Lockman Foundation. Used by permission.

Old Testament scripture quotations marked "AMP" are taken from *The Amplified Bible*, Old Testament. Copyright © 1965, 1987, by the Zondervan Corporation. Used by permission. All rights reserved.

Scripture quotations marked "ESV" are taken from *The Holy Bible, English Standard Version*. Copyright © 2000; 2001 by Crossway Bibles, a division of Good News Publishers. Used by permission. All rights reserved.

Scripture quotation marked "GW" is taken from *God's Word*. God's Word to the Nations. Grand Rapids, MI: Baker Publishing Group, 1995.

Scripture quotations marked "HCSB" are taken from the *Holman Christian Standard Bible*. Copyright © 1999, 2000, 2002, 2003, by Holman Bible Publishers. Used by permission.

Scripture quotations marked "KJV" are taken from the *Holy Bible, King James Version*. Cambridge, 1769.

Graeme Sellers is the lead pastor of Wonderful Mercy Church in Gilbert, Arizona. He serves on the national leadership team of the Alliance of Renewal Churches, an emerging network of kingdom-focused congregations sharing a Lutheran theological heritage and an identity as evangelical, Spirit-empowered, and sacramental. He is a member of the pastoral leadership team for PrayerQuake, an international bi-annual gathering focused on helping leaders and churches become contagious with a desire to pray more fervently and effectually. Graeme is an adjunct professor of theology for the Master's Institute Seminary in St. Paul, Minnesota. He has a bachelor's degree in history from Arizona State University and a master's of divinity from Fuller Theological Seminary. Graeme and his wife Jennifer have three lovely daughters and one very lively little boy.

14640589R00097

Made in the USA
Charleston, SC
22 September 2012